"Jamie has written a must-read for those looking for a story of hope in conquering strongholds in our lives. Discover practical biblical principles that will equip you to experience God's abundant plan for your life."
-Clair Hoover, *Executive Director – National Coalition of Ministries to Men*

"**Invincible** is a book that will encourage and uplift men in their desire to conquer the mountains of their lives. Jamie is the real deal. From his personal testimonies to his real life application of the biblical text, he provides a trail to follow that gives hope to others. He believes that if he can experience God's freedom and deliverance, then others can as well. I believe he is absolutely right. Read, study, share and grow. You will be blessed!"
-Stephen R. Tourville, D.Min. *PennDel Ministry Network Superintendent*

"On my white board in my office is the quote, "*Make defeat your fuel.*" Jamie has done that, he has taken 12 mountains that could have buried him and has instead conquered them and allowed them to fuel him to help other men find victory!

It has been my privilege to be both a mentor and friend to Jamie. I am proud of him and the energy he has invested in helping men grow. His newest book is a great resource to help men and men's small groups become **Invincible**"
-Tom Rees, *PennDel Ministry Network Men's Ministry Director*

"Jamie writes with an open heart exposing himself while giving men an opportunity to examine their own hearts. In his book, Jamie grapples with some of the toughest issues men face allowing them to come to terms with openness and frankness that eludes many men. Jamie's style and framework for this work is built for the men who

want to tackle the mountains they face with someone who has made the climb. This book will prove to be a great resource for men and a tremendous tool for men's groups."
-Bobby Basham, *Potomac Ministry Network Men's Ministry Director*

"Jamie describes in a personal way the challenges each man faces in life. He provides wise counsel on not only how to overcome these obstacles, but also how to have an even stronger relationship with Jesus because of them. When God uses the negative parts of life for a man's good, he becomes Invincible."
-Roy Smith, Ph.D., *psychologist, Author-Knights of the 21st Century*

"I believe that God honors bold prayers and is waiting to be invited on your expedition of faith. Invincible is a great tool to help you conquer the mountains that can so often stand in the way to answered prayers, miracles, and fulfilled dreams. This book will challenge you to step out to a place of powerful prayer, comfort, hope, and peace."
-Shawn Bentley, *Life Church of Hershey, Mantour Ministries/4One Ministries Board of Directors*

"I found Jamie's book refreshingly and brutally honest. He challenges men to face and deal with their issues while offering hope and how-tos. Everyone will face some of the mountains he mentions. Here is a guide for conquering and winning. I highly recommend it."
-Laverne Weber, *Victory's Journey*

"Jamie not only has a heart for men, but his message is timely for this generation. With raw transparency, he shares his story and lessons learned that lead men to freedom and victorious living. This book will be a blessing to any man or church looking to get real and to get free."
-Jason Tourville, *Lead Pastor Shrewsbury Assembly of God, Author*

"The term **Invincible** is applied to that which cannot be conquered in combat or war, nor overcome or subdued in any manner. Jamie shows men just that. That as men we can 'climb our mountains… claim our victory… and conquer the Mountains of anger, abuse, fear, shame and betrayal, through the power of the Spirit'. This powerful book is truly an insightful challenge to the reader. As an accomplished author, Jamie absolutely affirms a message of hope and victory as well as destiny. We can be **Invincible** through the power of the LORD! A must read."
-Walter G Smith, *Lead pastor of Abundant LIFE Church, South Central West sectional presbyter for the PennDel Ministry Network*

"The transparency portrayed in this amazing testimony is both refreshing, and life changing. **Invincible** will inspire, encourage, and minister to everyone, in all walks of life."
-Joey Cullen, *Director of the Greater Philadelphia Master's Commissions, 4One Ministries Board of Directors*

"Jamie Holden is filled with a passion to help men walk down some of the most difficult roads in their life. **Invincible** is a transparent look into his life and experiences and how he has gained freedom while facing mountain-sized obstacles that could have and/or should have crushed him. This glass house look into Jamie's life helps any reader connect to their own mountains in their life and gain insights from his experiences to see their own path to freedom."
-Jason Rising, *One18 Movement-Church Strategy/Health/Growth*

INVINCIBLE

Scaling The Mountains That Keep Us From Victory

James J. Holden
Founder, Mantour Ministries

Invincible: Scaling The Mountains That Keep Us From Victory

Published by 4One Ministries, Inc. Visit www.mantourministries.com for more information on bulk discounts and special promotions, or e-mail your questions to info@4oneministries.org.

Design: James J. Holden

The author wishes to recognize Adessa Holden for her contribution to the text as an integral part of 4One Ministries, Adessa has participated in numerous editorial sessions and has willing shared her words during the creation of this work to advance God's Kingdom.

Subject Headings:
1. Christian life 2. Men's Ministry 3. Spiritual Growth

ISBN 978-0-9988492-3-2
ISBN 978-0-9988492-4-9 (ebook)
Printed in the United States of America

DEDICATION

This book is dedicated to all those who pushed me, encouraged me, nudged me, nagged me, and supported me to write this book when I wasn't interested in reliving the painful memories of the past. Your unending perseverance is why this book is completed.

This book is also dedicated to the Mantour Conference Prayer Partners who held me up in prayer throughout the writing of this book. I truly could not have finished this project without your prayers through all the spiritual warfare and attacks that the enemy threw at me.

TABLE OF CONTENTS

-CHAPTER ONE-

YOU'VE STAYED HERE TO LONG!

"Nope, uh-uh, nada, not going to happen, never, no way, no how!"

I believe those were my exact words when it was first suggested that I write this particular book. You see, first my sister, then some fellow ministers, and finally my mentor, all without knowing the others had done it, suggested I work on a book where I shared my testimony of how God had set me free from so many areas of sin, bondage, and weakness. They all felt this book would help men overcome and experience the tremendous freedom that comes from God.

So why did I balk at the idea? Being 100% honest with you, I just didn't want to go back through all of it again and relive the pain. Life was good. God had done so much, and for the first time in years, I felt like my past was behind me, and I could move forward into the rest of my life.

Here's the problem: God doesn't just set us free so that we can be happy and ride off into the sunset. He sets us free so that we, in turn, can help other hurting, lost people find this same freedom and victory. By refusing to share my past, I was wasting this tremendous gift of freedom. So after prayer and finally surrendering my will, I sat down and wrote what you are about to read.

What finally changed my mind? Well, one day, I was doing my daily Bible reading, and I read the following passage of Scripture.

> *The Lord our God said to us at Horeb, "You have stayed long enough at this mountain. Break camp and advance into the hill country of the Amorites; go to all the neighboring peoples in the Arabah, in the mountains, in the western foothills, in the Negev and along the coast, to the land of the Canaanites and to Lebanon, as far as the great river, the Euphrates. See, I have given you this land. Go in and take possession of the land the Lord swore he would give to your fathers—to Abraham, Isaac and Jacob—and to their descendants after them."*
> *- Deuteronomy 1:6-8 NIV*

As I read this passage, these words in particular leaped off the page:

> *"You have stayed long enough at this mountain. Break camp and advance..."*

At that instance, God spoke to me and said, *"This is the word I want you to share with my men. Too many of my men came to me, accepted my salvation, but have yet to experience the complete freedom they can have in Christ. Their mountains are keeping them from moving forward."*

Then God said to me, *"I have set you free from so many mountains in your life...what right do you think you have to forget these victories? The pain of this time in your life is gone; now use these experiences to help other men find the same victory!"*

So that is what we are going to do in this book. We will begin by looking at this passage together, and in the following chapters we will look at the mountains that, not only I have faced, but many men face on a daily basis. I will share my story openly and honestly, no matter how embarrassing or shameful my past may be, and share with you how God helped me conquer these mountains in my life.

Let's start by looking at the passage again, this time in the Message version. I love the way the Message reads:

> *Back at Horeb, God, our God, spoke to us: "You've stayed long enough at this mountain. On your way now. Get moving".*

To fully understand this verse, we need to understand the backstory of this passage. The nation of Israel had been slaves in the land of Egypt for over 400 years. Daily they were beaten and abused. Someone else owned them. They had no say in their day to day lives. They had no freedom at all. But then God set them free!

God, through Moses, led the nation of Israel out of slavery in Egypt. The nation of Israel witnessed God's mighty salvation and deliverance. They daily ate manna given to them from God's hand. They walked on dry land across the Red Sea and saw the same sea swallow up and destroy their Egyptian enemies. They were given freedom and a new life from God.

The nation of Israel, well over a million people, made their way to God's holy mountain, Mt. Sinai. At Mount Sinai, they erected a tabernacle for God, God gave them the Ten Commandments, and they learned how to live free. However, while Mt Sinai was a holy place, a place for Israel to encounter God, it was not the Promised Land God had promised to give to the nation of Israel.

Their Promised Land was still out there waiting for them. Yes, it was inhabited by enemies who they would have to fight and destroy, but victory was promised to them.

You would expect them to be anxious to go and conquer their land, but as we just read in this passage, they were not. Instead, they got comfortable and settled in at Sinai for over two years.

God had so much more for His people than living all bunched together around this mountain. He saw they had much more potential inside of them. He was excited about the great blessing awaiting them. He knew that if the nation of Israel would just trust Him, obey Him, and serve Him, they would be invincible! Nothing or no one could defeat them. But first, they had to leave Mt. Sinai. The comfort of Mt. Sinai was keeping them from the victory and blessing in their Promised Land.

God had to give them a nudge and say, *"Seriously, you've stayed here at this mountain way too long. It's time to conquer this mountain and move into your Promised Land! Why settle for this when you could have so much more?!"*

I think these words ring true these thousands of years later. Too many of God's men came to Christ, accepted his salvation, but have yet to experience the complete freedom they can have in Christ. Their mountains are keeping them from moving forward.

Too many of God's men came to Christ, accepted his salvation, but have yet to experience the complete freedom they can have in Christ. Their mountains are keeping them from moving forward.

We all have mountains in our lives. These mountains, whether they are painful experiences, strongholds of sin, or areas of extreme weakness, are keeping us stuck in our walk with God. It is time we hear God's words and realize we weren't destined to stay at the base of these mountains, wallowing in the same pain, sin, and bondage we have endured for our entire lives. We are promised so much more! Freedom is there for the asking.

This reminds me of another Bible passage. This time it was the nation of Egypt, Israel's former oppressors, who were settling.

When God decided to set Israel free, He had to break Pharaoh's stubborn will, and He did this via ten plagues. Today, we're going to look at the second plague, frogs.

Reading in the book of Exodus, we see that God caused the entire nation of Egypt to be covered with frogs. Every inch of it had frogs over it. One encounter with Kermit the Frog is cute and funny, but dealing with millions of frogs must have been awful!

Let's look at this passage in Exodus 8:8-10:

> *Pharaoh summoned Moses and Aaron and said, "Pray to the Lord to take the frogs away from me and my people, and I will let your people go to offer sacrifices to the Lord."*
>
> *Moses said to Pharaoh, "I leave to you the honor of setting the time for me to pray for you and your officials and your people that you and your houses may be rid of the frogs, except for those that remain in the Nile."*
>
> *"Tomorrow," Pharaoh said.*
>
> *Moses replied, "It will be as you say, so that you may know there is no one like the Lord our God. The frogs will leave you and your houses, your officials and your people; they will remain only in the Nile." (NIV)*

I had read this passage so many times in my life, but a few years back I heard Pastor Glen Berteau speak at a men's conference. He focused on Pharaoh's reply, and he made a point that I had never thought about before, and it was so true. Look at Pharaoh's response again.

> *Moses said to Pharaoh, "I leave to you the honor of setting the time for me to pray for you and your officials and your people that you and your houses may be rid of the frogs, except for those that remain in the Nile."*
>
> *"Tomorrow," Pharaoh said.*

Tomorrow! Why did he wait until the following day to get rid of the frogs? Why was he willing to deal with them for another 24 hours? Why didn't he get them removed right away? He could

We as humans tolerate our mountains and our frogs way too much! God is calling us to more. He is saying, "You have stayed at your mountain too long!"

have been free of them that very minute, but he decides to tolerate them for 24 more hours!

Here's the truth:

We, as humans, tolerate our mountains and our frogs way too much! Freedom is there for us, but we decide to just accept things as they are. But God is calling us to more! He is saying, *"You have stayed at your mountain too long."*

• Your fears have stopped you long enough!

• Abuse has controlled you way too much!

• Your anger has controlled you far too long!

• Your shame has embarrassed you for too long!

• You have wallowed in your failure long enough!

• You are letting doubt keep you from moving forward!

• You are staying stuck in the aftermath of your broken relationships too long!

• You've allowed yourself to be mired in debt for long enough!

• You've let your physical limitations and sickness keep you down!

• You've nursed the wounds you received from betrayal too long!

On and on, the list goes. Our mountains are keeping us from being the husbands, the fathers, the leaders, the mentors, and the light to the world we were created to be. It's time we, as Christian men, hear God's voice and obey. It is time we conquer our mountains so we can become all God designed us to be. Freedom is available!

You can climb these mountains. You can claim victory! In Christ, YOU ARE INVINCIBLE!!

But you will never experience this if you stay at your mountain.

You must conquer it through the power of the Spirit.

I am a living testament to you today; you can conquer your mountain.

• Fear can be left behind as you're filled with godly courage.

• You can conquer the mountain of abuse and become a gentle, loving man.

• Your greatest shame that stands like a mountain in front of you can be your greatest testimony.

• You can leave your past failure behind and embrace your victorious life in Christ.

• Mt. Doubt can be defeated, and you can trust your Heavenly Father.

• Shattered relationships don't have to make you live alone forever.

• Your sickness doesn't have to define you any longer.

• You can permanently leave your addictions and bondages behind you.

• Betrayal can be replaced with good, solid relationships.

• Debt and money stress can be replaced with a life of good stewardship.

There is no mountain, no sin, no bondage, and no stronghold that the power of God can't overcome. Freedom is yours. You are invincible through the power of God.

But to experience this freedom, you have to first choose to leave your mountain behind and follow God into your Promised Land.

So that's where we begin this journey. Are you tired of being stuck in the same old sin and bondage? Are you sick of being mired in the same situations? Are you fed up with your past controlling your future?

If so, it's time to conquer your mountain and move forward into freedom. Let's begin the journey together.

CONTRACT BETWEEN YOU AND GOD
(AND YOUR MEN'S GROUP IF WORKING TOGETHER AS A GROUP)

Will you commit to:

Reading each chapter, including Scripture verses? Yes / No

Praying the prayers at the end of the chapter? Yes / No

Sincerely examining your heart using the questions at the end of each chapter? Yes / No

I,_____, am committed to conquering the mountains that keep me from freedom. I affirm this decision with my signature.

_____   _____

(Sign)   (Date)

Group Study Questions:

1. Which mountain in the list above jumped out to you the most?

2. Why do you think we tolerate our mountains and our frogs?

3. Are you willing to commit to climbing your mountains?

4. What spoke to you the most in this chapter?

5. After reading this chapter, what is one thing you will put into practice or one thing you will change in your life?

6. How can we, as a group, help you do this?

-CHAPTER TWO-

MT. FEAR

"I'm no longer a slave to fear; I am a child of God."[1]

I will never forget the first time I heard this worship song by Bethel Worship. Something inside me leapt as I heard words that so perfectly summed up my life.

You see, I have faced many mountains in my life, but the biggest mountain I had to conquer was Mt. Fear. I was a person who was absolutely consumed by fear.

I grew up in an abusive family. In my case, my dad was the abuser. His abuse caused me to be filled with fear, especially fear of men and men in authority. I spent a great deal of my life scared to death of being around men. That's a tough mountain to live with when God has called you to be a men's minister!

I still remember when God brought a man into my life who He wanted to mentor and disciple me. I was scared to death of this man when we first met. I was convinced he hated me! I remember one time I had set up my ministry display at an event, and when I saw this man coming down the hall towards where this display was set up, I literally hid under my table to avoid him! Fear consumed me!

This was not the only way I lived in fear. One of the biggest ways my dad abused me was by causing division between me and my mom. It was a classic abuser's move; turn a child against the parent who isn't abusing them to keep the secrets of the abuse hidden.

My dad would tell my mom how bad I was, how rebellious I was, etc., causing her to crack down on me to keep me in line as a parent should do. At the same time, he would tell me things like, "*You better keep quiet, if your mom finds out and we divorce, you will live with me. She doesn't want you. Look how hard she is on you.*"

He basically played us against each other. This is what is known today as Parent Alienation Syndrome. While there is a term for it now, when I was a child, all I knew was that it was my life, and I was consumed with fear and isolation. The one person I should have turned to was kept from me. I slowly became a terrified boy who was being consumed with fear, anger, hate, and rage.

Abuse was not the only way fear attacked me. I was born with a disability called Charcot-Marie-Tooth (CMT). It is a neurological disease that affected my limbs, deforming them. My hands are claw-like, and my feet are deformed outwards, causing me to basically walk on the sides of my feet. I couldn't tell you the last time the ball of my foot or the inside part of my foot touched the ground when I walked on my bad foot. Although I still struggle with it now, God completely healed my left foot, making it normal and healthy! However, for the first twenty years of my life, both my feet were deformed, causing me to constantly stumble, fall, and always be injured.

My disability consumed me with fear because I never knew when I would fall. I lived with the possibility that eventually I would end up in a wheelchair…would this be the year? I was terrified to be out walking at night because I wasn't able to run away if someone attacked me.

When I was seventeen, I got a job working at a store in Hersheypark. At the end of every shift, I had to count my cash register and take it to the office, which was a good half-mile from where I was stationed, and a good chunk of the trip was in a dark, empty area. I was always terrified of making this trip.

In grade school, I remember being bullied by an older high school kid who picked on me and pushed me around to impress his friends; he earned cheap respect from bullying a disabled kid half his age and size. There was a time when for some reason this guy and his friends came to my neighbor's house while I was outside playing, and I hid behind garbage cans and bushes so they wouldn't see me and come after me.

I was always filled with fear to go to new places and try new situations. When I was about twelve years old, the Christian school I went to all of my life closed down, and we had to go to a new school. I was so terrified on my first day that I cried like a four-year-old little girl in front of all the students and teachers. I was so out of control that they had to call my mom to come to the school. Talk about making a first impression! But I was consumed by fear.

These are just a few examples of the fears that consumed me. But then one day, God said to me, *"You have stayed at this mountain of fear too long. I want to set you free."*

I had to allow the Holy Spirit to begin showing me the areas of fear in my life. I had to remember the times of abuse, the painful experiences, and the feelings of insecurity that allowed the fear to enter my life. I am not going to lie to you and say it was easy and pain-free. It was hard to remember these times. But God's promise of freedom was worth the pain, and He kept His promise to help me through and overcome.

I had to forgive those who had contributed to the fear, like my father for his abuse, and bullies in school who had been cruel to me.

For me, fear was such a serious thing that it actually developed a stronghold in my life. Strongholds are areas where Satan has established control. They are areas of frequent temptations that are so strong they result in feelings of failure, hopelessness, and defeat.

Victories never lasted.[2] That's what my fear was like in my life.

I was literally consumed by fear from which God delivered me. I had to renounce the fear and its effects. I had to pray and order the fears to leave my life and stay out in Jesus' name. I had to accept God's call to freedom, and conquer Mt. Fear. And God set me free!

Now I live fearlessly! My life changed when I conquered Mt. Fear. I am no longer a slave to fear! I am living in God's Promised Land.

Strongholds are areas where Satan has established control. They are areas of frequent temptations that are so strong they result in feelings of failure, hopelessness, and defeat.

Remember the man I hid under the table from? He is now my Missionary Supervisor, mentor, and one of my closest friends, a man I trust implicitly. I am living my dream, ministering to men and helping them gain victory in their lives.

None of it would have been possible if I stayed bound in fear at the base of Mt. Fear.

• I never could have stood in front of a crowd to speak.

• I never could have ministered one-on-one with men.

• I never could have started a new ministry.

• I never could have started my life over at the age of 39 and become an Assemblies of God United States Missionary, dependent on the help of friends and churches to financially support me. I never could have trusted God to be my sole source of income as I raised my support, living on $500 a month. And trust me, this is still the biggest battle I face as fear tries to use this to re-enter my life!

On and on the list goes of victories and blessings I have experienced from God because I finally stopped wallowing in fear and terror and conquered Mt. Fear!

The same freedom is there for you! You do not need to be a slave to fear any longer.

"But Jamie, you don't understand! The situations in my life causing the fear are real. I don't know if I can overcome."

I understand. People are losing their jobs. Finances are tightening, and 401K's are shrinking. We worry if we will have good healthcare or if we will lose it. Relationships are tested. We fear sickness or poor health. On and on the list goes.

We can even struggle with fear in our relationship with God. He may ask us to do something or make a change in our life, and the thought of the change terrifies us. As we go through these times, we often feel worried and afraid. Fear is a natural reaction in tough times.

However, God's will is for you to break the grip fear has on you and embrace his freedom. I am not saying it is easy. Fear can be a crippling emotion. However, there is hope. We can conquer our fears and continue moving forward with God to face our giants. I know this fact firsthand. I broke free from fear and so can you!

God's will is for you to break the grip fear has on you and embrace his freedom.

So what are some ways we can conquer Mt. Fear?

1. Admit The Mountain Exists

I know, Captain Obvious strikes again. But this is an important step! You won't conquer the mountain until you admit it is there.

As men, it is embarrassing to admit we are afraid. We're tough, manly men. Guess what, we still have fear. Even the bravest guys like John Wayne face fear in their life. What makes them brave is that even though they experience fear, they know they can't stay there, paralyzed by it. As John Wayne once said, *"Courage is being scared to death, but saddling up anyway."*

2. Get to the Root of the Fear

After we admit we are battling fear, we need to figure out the cause of the fear. When did it start? What were you doing? What was going on around you?

For me, to conquer my fear I had to realize the fear stemmed from both my abusive childhood and my disability. For you, it will be something different.

I had to face the memories of my abuse and the fear my disability caused. I had to forgive my abusers, and I even had to choose to forgive God for creating me with my disability.

We all need to examine ourselves to see what fears we have allowed to cripple us and keep us from becoming all God wants us to be.

3. Reach Out To God for Victory

Daily ask God for His courage and for the ability to trust Him to take care of you. Memorize some Scriptures on fear to help you fight. Here are a few to get you started:

> *For God has not given us a spirit of fear, but of power and of love and of a sound mind. - 2 Tim. 1:7 (NKJV)*

> *Don't panic. I'm with you. There's no need to fear for I'm your God. I'll give you strength. I'll help you. I'll hold you steady, keep a firm grip on you. - Isaiah 41:10 (The Message)*

> *Be strong and courageous. Do not be afraid or terrified because of them, for the Lord your God goes with you; he will never leave you nor forsake you. -Deuteronomy 31:6 (NIV)*

Pray these verses. God's Word is full of promises to His sons that give us strength and encouragement to overcome our fears.

4. Daily Pray For Godly Courage

Be strong and very courageous. Be careful to obey all the law my servant Moses gave you; do not turn from it to the right or to the left, that you may be successful wherever you go. Keep this Book of the Law always on your lips; meditate on it day and night, so that you may be careful to do everything written in it. Then you will be prosperous and successful. Have I not commanded you? Be strong and courageous. Do not be afraid; do not be discouraged, for the Lord your God will be with you wherever you go."
- Joshua 1:7-9 (NIV)

A man can never realize his full potential in God's kingdom until he comes to the place where he is willing to conquer his fears and be strong and courageous. Our world is crying out for men who will be strong and courageous! Your fear can be replaced with godly courage.

5. Don't Be Afraid to Ask for Help

For me, victory came with the help of a Christian counselor who also understood spiritual warfare. He helped me realize fear had developed into a stronghold in my life, allowing me to pray until the stronghold was broken. The crippling fear was defeated by the power of the Holy Spirit once and for all.

In order to enter into the Promised Land God has for you, you must defeat Mt. Fear.

Fear keeps you from moving forward, while courage brings you victory. You've stayed at Mt. Fear too long. It's not God's will for you. Let's end by looking at this verse in Isaiah 43:1-4:

But now, God's Message... "Don't be afraid, I've redeemed you. I've called your name. You're mine. When you're in over your head, I'll be there with you. When you're in rough waters, you will not go down. When you're between a rock and a hard place, it won't be a dead end—Because I am God, your personal God, The Holy of Israel, your Savior.

I paid a huge price for you…. That's how much you mean to me! That's how much I love you! I'd sell off the whole world to get you back, trade the creation just for you." (The Message)

God cares about you so much. He will never leave you. When you boldly step forward and conquer Mt. Fear, you can do so knowing He will be right there with you, fighting for you, protecting you, and giving you the victory!

Dear Heavenly Father,

You know the struggle with fear I have had in my life. You know my fears, the terror that is crippling me and causing me to not reach my full potential in you. Give me the strength and courage to face this fear. Help me to destroy it once and for all.

Thank you for your continued presence in my life, helping me to devour this fear. Help me to trust in your power to deliver me from my fears.

In Jesus' name, Amen.

GROUP STUDY QUESTIONS:

1. What is an area of fear that keeps you from moving forward?

2. What is a stronghold? Can you recognize any strongholds in your life?

3. When did your fear start? What caused it?

4. How can prayer and Bible reading help you conquer Mt. Fear?

5. After reading this chapter, what is one thing you will put into practice or one thing you will change in your life?

6. How can we, as a group, help you do this?

-CHAPTER THREE-

MT. SICKNESS

I remember the first time I realized I was different. I was seven years old and heading to my first Little League practice. Up until this time, I had only played ball in the safety and solitude of my backyard with my dad. But this was different.

Because kids are kids, it was quickly pointed out to me that I walked funny and ran even funnier...and slower. Until this point, I never knew I had a disability. Now I knew; I wasn't like the other kids.

My mom never wanted me to play organized sports. She knew I physically couldn't do it and wanted to spare me the pain of the ridicule and scorn that rained down every game. I was one of the best hitters on our team, but because of my disability, I couldn't run, and was often teased and ridiculed by the other team, my own teammates, and even parents in the stands. (This was in the days before participation trophies and rules restricting heckling from the grandstands.) Even my own coach was tough and borderline cruel to me because of my lack of abilities. Eventually, I quit the team.

My disability is something I have dealt with my entire life. As I said in the last chapter, I was born with a neurological disease named Charcot-Marie-Tooth (CMT). It is a degenerative nerve disease. It weakens bones and muscles and causes limb deformation. It is a hereditary disease passed down from generation to generation. My grandpa had it, my dad has it, and I am still dealing with it to this day. Unless God intervenes, it will get worse with the passing of time, and eventually I could end up in a wheelchair.

I would be lying to tell you it had no effect on my life. It was a HUGE mountain I had to face on a daily basis. My dad couldn't handle the fact that he had this disability, and, for most of his life, he ignored it and pretended it didn't exist. He did the same with me and my disability, but the CMT had more dramatic effects on my body and was more severe. However, he acted like it didn't exist, and I quickly learned it was best if I did the same. Still, it did exist.

When I was about nine, the Christian school I went to decided it was a good idea to have all the students take gym class together. Let me tell you, a healthy nine year old kid can't compete in flag football with an eighteen year old, worse yet, a disabled nine year old. To add insult to injury, the field we played on was two miles from the school, and the gym teacher decided it would be good for us to run there and run back.

Only I couldn't run.

I remember the older guys would run at lightning speed until they were out of sight and then walk the rest of the way, taking shortcuts through a farmer's field. But I was always the last one running, with the gym teacher acting like a drill sergeant barking in my ear to run faster, do better, etc. But I couldn't.

One day I decided I was going run as fast as I could to start off and try and get ahead of the gym teacher. I ran as hard as I could, but my ankle rolled, I fell and smacked my head on a sewage pipe sticking out of the ground. Blood gushed from my head, and I needed a ton of stitches. But worse than that, I grew angrier, more emotionally damaged, and I crawled even further inside of myself. I hated my body, and I grew angry with God for making me this way!

When I turned twelve, my dad decided it was time for me to get a job to earn money, and he found me jobs mowing people's lawns. While it was good for me to learn the value of hard work and earning money, I physically shouldn't have done this job. With my foot deformation, I couldn't walk on grass or uneven surfaces without rolling my ankles, so for most of my summers I had swollen and sprained ankles, causing further damage to my nerves and ligaments.

Around the age of fourteen, I sprained my ankle really badly and had to go to an orthopedic surgeon. Around this same time, I transferred to yet another school. (I did handle it better than the first time I mentioned in the Mt. Fear chapter...but then again, I couldn't have handled it worse!) The orthopedic surgeon was a young doctor, fresh out of medical school, and he was the first to actually diagnose me with CMT, which at that time was a rare, unheard-of, newly-discovered disease.

This doctor felt he could perform a new type of operation where they cut a huge hunk of bone out of your instep, causing the foot to reform normally. Anxious to be normal like all the other guys my age, we agreed to have both feet operated on, separately, of course. So I was at a new school with new kids, and my disability took center stage as I had operations, casts, and months of recovery.

The surgeries weren't very successful. Because the disease was degenerative, the bones slowly started deforming again.

My self-worth was formed on those early days of Little League, and over the years I became angrier and more sullen. For most of my early life and adulthood, I felt inferior, like less of a man and not as good as everyone else. While my disability limited me physically, it really crippled me emotionally.

I would become outraged whenever anyone asked me a simple question about my disability. I took concern and curiosity as attacks against me and my manhood. Anyone who dared to bring it up would never do it again after experiencing my wrath!

Even while in college I struggled with these feelings of inferiority. One weekend at college, the guys and I were having a good time together. On Friday night we went out for a late night Denny's run, and then the next day we played video games all day. One of the games we played was a racing game where you street raced while cops tried to catch you. We loved this game.

Then my one friend had to leave for work that evening, and when he left, for some reason, he tried to squeal out like you do in the video game. However, he had an old car and blew his transmission! He came back to the dorm and asked a bunch of us to help him push his car back. Now, I should have said "No" because I physically couldn't do it, but I would never have made such a concession, so I went along to help.

I struggled to keep up with the guy as we walked the mile to where the car broke down. It got worse when we got there. We pushed it up the hill, but when we got to the top, someone suggested we just get it started down the hill, and then all jump in and ride it down.

All the guys pushed, and as the car started rolling down the hill, they jumped in. I struggled to run to catch the car, and as I tried to hop in, I tripped, fell, and skinned my legs and knees. But even worse, my pride was hurt. I pulled inside of myself and retreated to the solitude of my room, spending the rest of the weekend alone, angry, and dying inside.

Around this time, I went to a service geared around healing. The speaker was a nationally-known healing minister. Stories of people being healed were shown daily on his TV show. What they didn't show on TV were the hundreds of people being brought to him in wheelchairs and hospital beds only to be wheeled back out at the end, still suffering physically. Never having seen this side, I went to this meeting convinced I would be healed of my disability.

When the time for the altar call came, one of the minister's helpers came up to me and said they had a word from God that I was going to be healed of a problem with my foot. I leaped inside with joy. I knew this was going to happen! But as soon as they spoke the words, they said, *"Oh I'm sorry, it's not you. It's the man behind you."* The man walked to the stage and was healed.

I was devastated.

The one thing I wanted more than anything else was presented to me, and then snatched away.

I became so angry with God that night. Why couldn't He have healed me? That night started a downward spiral of anger and self abuse as I lashed out at God and my disability.

When I was a sophomore in college, I got really sick. I ended up being rushed home, and eventually ended up in the hospital. Little did I know, my semester ended that day. I ended up in the emergency room with a raging temperature of 105 degrees. Vomiting and hemorrhaging uncontrollably, the doctors told my parents they didn't expect me to make it.

I remember the worst of this ordeal. It was the night before my 20th birthday. My fever spiked higher, and doctors feared that even if I lived, I'd have permanent brain damage. My entire body was packed in ice. I was dying. I remember praying to God the only prayer I had the strength to pray. I said, *"Daddy, help me, I can't do this on my own."*

You need to understand, I never referred to God as *"daddy"* in my life. He was Lord, not father. I had too many issues with my own dad to look at God through those eyes. But as soon as I spoke those words, I heard God say, *"You're going to be ok. I am here to help you."*

The next day I woke up and my fever broke. God had completely healed me!

Not only that, but he also healed my left foot. There was no trace of CMT in it! It was a normal, healthy foot. I had to regain my strength after losing 35 lbs in 6 days, and I had to go through physical therapy to learn to walk again, but eventually I was released, and I went home. The doctor said there was no brain damage, (I know some who know me may not believe that to be true! LOL), and I was even able to take my finals that I had missed. I even had the best GPA that semester I ever had.

You would think this experience would have changed me and my issues with my body. But to be honest, it didn't. Instead of being happy that God healed my one foot, I was angry He didn't heal both. I pulled away from God and others even more and abused my body like never before, burying the pain I felt, in denial.

After I graduated, I ended up moving back home. I had abused my body so badly that my bad foot was basically unwalkable. I was trapped back in the house I never wanted to go back to, stuck living with my father who had now reached the peak of his abusive behavior after the death of his dad, and I was too injured to do anything about it.

Around this time, I was helping my dad put an air conditioner unit in a window. As we installed it, it slipped from my dad's hands. Instinctively, I reached out and grabbed it.

Instantly, I felt excruciating pain in my back and ribs. The cartilage that connects the ribs to the spine had torn, and the pain was excruciating.

I suffered from this injury for over a year. This new injury, along with living with an abusive dad, coming back home after college, and other issues, caused me to sink into a deep depression. For over a year, I rarely left the house, combed my hair, or took care of myself physically. I gained over 50 pounds and sunk deep into depression. I was mired at the foot of Mt. Sickness, and I gave up fighting to climb this mountain.

Eventually, my mom had enough of my behavior and called me out for giving up. She sternly helped me see that I was in deep trouble and needed to make changes. I had to get back up and start living again.

For the first time in my life, I was ready to deal with the pain in my life. I had to once and for all deal with the anger I felt towards God for giving me my disability. I had to face the painful memories of events I told you about in this chapter and allow God to heal my emotions.

God started showing me that my disability didn't make me less of a man. It didn't even have to define me. God gave me a list of what a real man is according to His Word. I worked through the pain of my past, the pain of my disability. With the help of the Holy Spirit, I was able to forgive all of those who treated me so badly and abused me, and I was able to forgive God for creating me the way He did.

Then, I asked God to forgive me and make me into a new man. Even though I physically wasn't healed, I was able to climb Mt. Sickness and conquer that mountain.

We can't change our disability, sickness, or disease, but we can change how we react to them and allow them to influence our lives.

How did I do it? Well, it started with me bringing my feelings about my disability to God. But I also learned a few steps that I believe will help you to also conquer Mt. Sickness. We can't change our disability, sickness, or disease, but we can change how we react to it and allow it to influence our lives.

1. Be a Victor, not a Victim

As someone who spent most of his life living with a victim mentality, I get how easy it is to fall into this trap. I learned at an early age how to play the victim and use my disability. I would manipulate people with my sickness, use it to control people, and guilt people into doing what I wanted. Basically, I played the victim card to get what I wanted.

This was so wrong. As Christians, we can't live as victims. It is not healthy. In reality, if you are a Christian who is also battling Mt. Sickness, it can be lead you to adopt sinful attitudes through your victim mentality.

"Ouch, Jamie! You're saying I am a sinner because I am sick?"

Of course not! I didn't say your sickness was sin; I said having a victim mentality about your sickness can cause you to fall into a sinful mindset. Why?

Salvation and freedom in Christ are amazing gifts for us, and the joy of this salvation and the freedom we are given in Christ should make us so grateful to God that we will endure anything else life throws at us, including sickness.

It wasn't until I adopted this attitude that I could start scaling Mt. Sickness. I had to stop feeling like the victim and stop using my disease to abuse and control others. I chose to take on the attitude that, even if I had my disability for the rest of my life, that was okay. God had saved me and set me free, and if He wanted me to have this disability, my job was to endure with a good attitude. I had to stop being a victim and start living a victorious life in Christ. The same is true for you.

2. Be Better; not Bitter

I have come to learn a simple fact: Very few people will look down on a disabled person or refuse to be around them or like them…however, NO ONE likes being around a bitter person!

People will not reject you for your sick body, but they will reject you if you have a bitter heart!

> Very few people will look down on a disabled person or refuse to be around them or like them… however, NO ONE likes being around a bitter person!

We can't live as angry, bitter people who let our anger and unforgiveness towards God continue in our lives. We need to ask God to forgive us and help us to not be a bitter person, but a better person…a person who treats people with love.

Like I said before, I couldn't climb Mt. Sickness until I dealt with my anger with God. I was angry with God that He gave me CMT, and I was furious with Him that He wouldn't take it away. I had to deal with this anger. I had to repent. I had to pray and ask God to take my anger and bitterness away. I had to stop being bitter, and instead be better.

3. Don't Let Your Sickness Be Your Identity

When I was a kid, I loved a television show called, *"Battle of the Network Stars,"* especially when they would have episodes with athletes battling, like NFL players from the AFC vs NFL players from the NFC. I thoroughly enjoyed watching these amazing athletes battle on the obstacle course or the tug of war.

Recently, ABC rebooted *Battle of the Network Stars*, and, of course, I had to watch. One of the weeks they had a contestant who has Multiple Sclerosis. The sideline reporter commented how amazing it was that this contestant would be willing to do this rugged course with MS. The contestant said something very profound. He answered, *"MS lives with me, I don't live with MS."*

What a great attitude! I have personally come to live with this attitude. If I lived with CMT, I would never leave the house! For a year of my life, I didn't leave the house. If I lived with CMT, there would be no Mantour Conferences. I wouldn't be traveling around speaking. I wouldn't be writing books. Men in prisons wouldn't be ministered to by the books I have written. I don't mean this arrogantly; I am just showing that if I gave into the pain that I feel, life wouldn't be happening.

Personally, I'd never have the joy of going jet skiing, going to a store, or having fun. But I don't live with CMT, CMT lives with me!

I have learned to not let my sickness define me. I have overcome my insecurities, feelings of inferiority, and embarrassment. For instance, last week, we had to buy a new refrigerator. I could have stayed in the car and wallowed in how my CMT hurt too badly to walk in the store. Instead, I humbled myself to use one of the electric wheelchair carts and roll around the store.

I had a blast flying around the aisles, honking the horn, and laughing the entire time. I NEVER could have done this or enjoyed this if I stayed camped at the foot of Mt. Sickness, but I conquered this mountain and stopped letting my sickness be my identity. My identity is in Christ!

4. Allow God's Glory to Shine Through Your Weakness

We can't allow anger with God to cause us to become discontent with or demanding of God. As Corrie Ten Boom once said, *"Don't bother to give God instructions, just report for duty."* We need to take this attitude with Mt. Sickness.

I need to share some cold-hard facts with you. God does what He thinks is best.

1. Sometimes God heals us.

2. Sometimes He doesn't.

3. He always does what is best for His kingdom through our bodies.

God will heal you if it is best for His kingdom, and He won't heal you if it isn't the best thing for His kingdom. It isn't about you, it's about Him.

God will heal you if it is best for His kingdom, and He won't heal you if it isn't the best thing for His kingdom. It isn't about you, it's about Him. If He can use you more not healed, than He won't heal you.

Another great quote from Corrie Ten Boom sums this up perfectly. *"Every experience God gives us, every person he puts in our lives is the perfect preparation for the future that only he can see."* This includes our battles with sickness, disease and pain.

I had to accept this fact in my life. I had to say to God,

"I will surrender my will to yours.

You are allowing this CMT to remain inside of my body.

You are allowing every step I take to feel like someone is stabbing me in the foot repeatedly.

You are allowing me to have excruciating pain while I stand to speak.

You are allowing it because you are using my weakness to shine your glory. You're using it to encourage and inspire other people. I know when I am of more use to the kingdom healed than I am unhealed, you will heal me, but for now the kingdom is better served with me having this disability."

It was a hard place to come to in my life, yet it was very freeing. It allowed me to refocus my attention on God and off of my disability. It helped me accept the disability and learn to not have it define my identity. I now see my disability as a tool to grow God's kingdom.

The Apostle Paul understood this truth. Look at his words on Mt. Sickness:

> *I was given the **gift of a handicap** to keep me in constant touch with my limitations. Satan's angel did his best to get me down; what he in fact did was push me to my knees. No danger then of walking around high and mighty! At first I didn't think of it as a gift, and begged God to remove it. Three times I did that, and then he told me,*
>
> *My grace is enough; it's all you need. My strength comes into its own in your weakness.*
>
> *Once I heard that, I was glad to let it happen. **I quit focusing on the handicap and began appreciating the gift.** It was a case of Christ's strength moving in on my weakness. Now I take limitations in stride, and with good cheer, these limitations that cut me down to size—abuse, accidents, opposition, bad breaks. I just let Christ take over! And so **the weaker I get, the stronger I become.** -2 Corinthians 12:7-10 (The Message, emphasis mine)*

You don't know whose life you will reach or what lives will be

When you make your greatest weakness into God's greatest strength through you, lives will be changed, and God's kingdom will grow.

changed as they see you conquer Mt. Sickness. When you make your greatest weakness into God's greatest strength through you, lives will be changed and God's kingdom will grow.

We will be better equipped to help hurting people because of our pain. Our sickness will help refine us and remove sins and weaknesses, making us more like Jesus. It can make us into more compassionate people. Who knows? Your pain could be the very thing that reaches someone and brings them into God's Kingdom!

Paul got this, and he conquered Mt. Sickness. So can you!

Dear Heavenly Father,

You know the sickness, the physical pain, the disease, or disability that I live with everyday. Father, I don't want to stay at the foot of Mt. Sickness any longer.

Forgive me for any times I have allowed my sickness to make me into a victim or bitter. Forgive me for allowing my identity to be in my physical issues instead of in you. Help me come to the place where I can surrender my will and my physical limitations to you so that your kingdom can be grown through my weakness, knowing that you will heal me if it will better the kingdom. Help me, like Paul, to rejoice in my weakness and conquer Mt. Sickness. In Jesus Name, Amen!

GROUP STUDY QUESTIONS:

1. In this chapter, we said, *"Be a victor not a victim."* What did this mean to you?

2. Why is removing bitterness important to climbing Mt. Sickness?

3. How can God use your weakness to build His kingdom?

4. How can prayer and Bible reading help you conquer Mt. Sickness?

5. After reading this chapter, what is one thing you will put into practice or one thing you will change in your life?

6. How can we, as a group, help you do this?

–CHAPTER FOUR–

MT. ABUSE

People often ask me why I decided to become a men's minister. Even though it is fulfilling and you see some of the greatest testimonies and results come from men selling out to God, it is also one of the hardest, most discouraging and frustrating types of ministry to do. It is not for the faint of heart!

My answer, other than the fact that God called me to do this ministry, is that God has done so much in my life and given me such amazing freedom in Him. I want to help men experience this same freedom! My passion is to see men become strong, godly men--- becoming all they can be in God's kingdom.

You see, that is the reason I do what I do, not so there can be more programs or activities. I am not into building new programs. I am all about seeing changed lives in our churches' men, and I believe discipleship and men's ministry is key.

My passion in life is to see God's men become sold-out, on-fire men of God. I want to see men stand up and become godly husbands and fathers.

I long to see men leave their old way of life behind them and become, strong mature men of God. I ache to see men become leaders in their homes, their churches, and their communities.

But more than anything else, I want men to experience the tremendous freedom that is rightfully theirs from sin and bondage in their lives.

My dream is that all men will be able to see the huge mountains in their life and know that, with God's help, they can overcome! I want them to experience God setting them free and making them into a new creation. Why? Because God did it in my life, and I want my brothers to experience the same peace, joy, and freedom that can only be found in Christ.

One of the biggest mountains that God set me free from is a huge mountain that so many men struggle with in their lives…abuse. Too many men struggle with being abusive. Most of these men are abusive because they have faced abuse in their own lives.

Abuse is a huge mountain, but it can be conquered! Trust me, I know firsthand.

(Before I share my story, I want to start by saying that I do not share this out of anger or to get back at my dad. He is well aware of what I am about to share, and he has given me permission to share our story if it will help other men destroy the abuse in their lives.)

I grew up in the church. My mom became a Christian when I was still in diapers. She grew up in an abusive family situation, and she always struggled to feel loved. She married my dad, but because of his own abusive childhood, he wasn't capable of showing her love. He wasn't really ready to get married and take on the responsibility of caring for a wife and family, but because it was socially acceptable to get married at a certain age and it was very important to his family to keep up the appearance that everything was normal and healthy (even perfect), he got married.

Their early years of marriage were rough. My mom told my sister and me, when we were older, that she went for a car ride one night after one of their fights. She was on a windy mountain road, and she seriously considered just letting go of the steering wheel and letting the car crash down over the mountain. However, she just couldn't do it because she knew there would be no one to raise Adessa and me. Her love for us outweighed the torment she lived on a daily basis.

One day, our neighbor asked my mom to come with her to the local Pentecostal church. My mom went, and when the altar call came, she went forward and accepted Jesus as her Savior. Her life was instantly changed. She told us that this was the first time in her life she ever felt like someone loved her and wanted her. She fell in love with God that day, and she sold out completely to Him.

She eventually got my dad to come to church with her. Week after week, he would sit through the service, but as the end approached and it got closer to the altar call, he would take me out to the nursery so he wouldn't have to respond. One Sunday, for some reason, he didn't get to make his great escape. As the altar call was given, the man sitting behind my dad put his arm on his shoulder and said to him, *"You're going to that altar because you need Jesus!"*

Now this guy was well-known to my dad. His name was Louie, and he was an old drinking buddy of my dad's grandfather. They were big, burly men, coal miners who spent their nights drinking, brawling, gambling and womanizing. Their stories were legendary, such as my great grandfather gambling away the family business or Louie busting up the town bar again in another brawl.

Now Louie was a changed man. He had a dramatic conversion. He went dry, he left his old friends behind, and he was a born-again Christian. He was one of the few people who knew my dad's family secrets, and he knew my dad needed Jesus. So he forcefully led him to the altar and made him say a sinner's prayer.

Now, while effective, I don't recommend this approach. Why? Because my dad went to the altar out of fear, not from the Holy Spirit's conviction. Louie meant well, but to be honest, all he did was create a big mess. Why?

Because my dad wasn't serious about becoming a Christian. My dad was only interested in one thing, keeping all of his secrets hidden about the horrible abuse he endured growing up. Church and Christianity became another veneer covering up all of the damage inside of him. It was one more thing he used to cover it up. But it wasn't a genuine conversion.

Because my dad was an accountant and because he gave the impression that he was a good, upstanding man, he quickly became a leader in the church. He was made a board member. Suddenly, my dad had the respect and admiration he always wanted in life. However, he wasn't receiving the one thing he needed more than anything…a group of strong, godly men discipling and mentoring him.

Because of this, my dad never changed. He just had the shiny new, morally upright disguise of a good church man to cover all the damage in his heart and the sins that resulted from them. While everyone else saw the nice, Christian man, behind closed doors my dad was an angry, controlling, and abusive man.

His anger dominated his life; he controlled us all and everything we did to make sure we kept up the appearance of the perfect family that he wanted so badly growing up. When we failed to portray the image of perfection, which happened quite often because, let's face it, no one is perfect, abuse was used to keep us in line. He abused my mom in every way possible. He was extremely emotionally and verbally abusive with all of us, and from time to time, he was physically abusive towards me. But his favorite weapon he used to beat and abuse us with was his Bible.

How do you beat someone with the Bible?

Well, my dad was a master at twisting and manipulating the Scripture. He misused the verses on being submissive and wives submitting to their husbands, children submitting, etc. I am sure you know what I am talking about. He used these verses to condone his abusive treatment of us.

One of the biggest ways my dad abused me was by causing division between me and my mom. We discussed this in the fear chapter. But it had a HUGE impact on my early life, causing me to become a scared and angry young man.

Another huge issue that caused abuse in our family came because of physical issues. Part of my dad's need to keep everything perfect meant that sickness was not allowed. He saw sickness and health issues as a sign of weakness and as imperfection. However, my mom and sister both had physical issues, and I had my disability.

As I mentioned earlier, I was born with a neurological disease that twists and distorts limbs. It is a hereditary disease. My father and grandfather had it as well. My dad refused to admit he had the disease and lived as if it didn't exist. He absolutely couldn't stand the guilt that it was passed on to me, and to cover this pain, he acted like it didn't exist. But it did.

Because of my dad's abuse, I slowly began to become a boiling pot of anger, rage, and hatred and was consumed with fear. I was a mess. I rebelled against my mom and her ways. She received the brunt of what I felt for my dad.

After I graduated high school, I felt God call me to ministry, so I enrolled at the University of Valley Forge. I packed up all of my bags, including all my emotional baggage and wounds, and headed off to prepare for a life of ministry.

I LOVED college. For the first time in my life, I was free of my dad's abuse as well as my mom's strict rules. I lived it up big time in college. I had fun staying up late, sleeping in, watching all the TV shows and movies I wasn't allowed to watch growing up and playing the video games we weren't allowed to have. College was like a four-year freedom party. However, all my baggage was still with me.

Because of my physical disability and the abuse, I always struggled with feeling like I wasn't good enough. I didn't feel like I was as good as the other guys. In my own eyes, I didn't measure up to them. I constantly felt the need to prove my manhood. In order to fit in, I began setting aside my convictions and compromising to be one of the guys.

At the same time though, I was deeply involved with the men's ministry on campus. However, like my dad, I didn't deal with any of my issues, and instead embraced the image others had of me. I became one of the leaders. I would lead a group on campus, and then when the meeting ended and the guys left, I would go back to my room and watch pornography.

I was a huge hypocrite. I am not making excuses, but I didn't think that what I was doing was wrong. I grew up with a dad who lived this way, and everyone said he was such a man of God. I really honestly believed I was ok with God. Not only that, but I felt I was going to be the next Billy Graham!

Thankfully, during this time, God brought a godly professor into my life who, for some reason, took an interest in me. He somehow saw that I was struggling to survive spiritually, and he decided to mentor me. I will forever be grateful for him in my life. He became the friend and mentor I needed. He slowly began showing me through how he lived his life that my image of a godly man was all wrong.

Meanwhile, things fell apart at home. My dad began having flashback memories of his abusive childhood, and he couldn't handle it. The godly, perfect father that I thought I had, began to get violent and angry.

Things in our home began to deteriorate. From being around the godly professors at college, I had been seeing for a while that the godly father I grew up with was a farce. Of course, growing up there had been physical, mental and emotional abuse, but we were told that it was our fault and my mom's fault and we deserved it. Now, seeing real men and the way they acted, my dad didn't line up.

Then we discovered my father had been living a secret life. He had accumulated a huge secret debt that he kept hidden for years. (We'll discuss this more in out chapter 9.) To this day, we really don't know what the money was spent on. The exposure of his secret life plus the memories and flashbacks he was having turned my dad into a violent man.

Around this time, I graduated college. I vowed in my heart that I was done with all the pain and drama of life back home. I was on my way to being a great evangelist; I was never going home again. Well, guess where God took me after graduation?

That's right. I tried every door possible to find a ministry position, but nothing opened up for me. At the same time, I seriously injured my bad foot and could barely walk. I had nowhere to go but the one place I never wanted to go...home.

So at the age of twenty-two, I moved back home with my family, sure it was only a matter of time before I would move out to become the next celebrity minister. However, God had other plans.

During this time, my dad's rage issues grew. There were times I had to get between him and my mom. I remember once he was doing something with a cooking knife, and my sister upset him. I had to jump between him and her as he came at her, knife in hand. Another time during a fit of rage, he came after me, and my mom stepped between us. He threw her into the bookshelf, bruising a few of her ribs. During this time, I would sleep with a baseball bat, and my mom and sister would sleep with rolling pins. It was a nightmare!

Slowly, anger and rage consumed me. I was furious at God for making me live like this. Why couldn't I have a ministry position and leave this madness behind? Hatred for my dad consumed me, and slowly, I turned into him.

Yet, the whole time, God was waiting for me to face all the issues inside of me. But just like dad, I refused and pushed them aside.

I loved God and wanted to serve Him. I knew I was called to the ministry, but I didn't realize that call couldn't happen until I dealt with my sin, my addictions, and my rage. I was stuck in a mad cycle of loving and serving God, followed by outbursts of anger and rage, and then repentance and promises it would never happen again. But it just kept happening! Just like my dad.

Finally the mad cycle came to a head in my life. I'll never forget that night. I woke up in the middle of the night to a blood curling scream. My mom had a nightmare that scared her so badly that she jumped out of bed to run away. As she jumped up, she tripped and fell, injuring her shoulder. Scared, half-asleep, and in pain, she screamed for help. My sister and I jumped out of bed, ran to her side, and helped her.

At this point, my dad put in his two cents. He was angry at my mom for waking him. He showed no concern for her or her health. Instead, he verbally and emotionally abused this woman in pain.

His behavior infuriated me. I was so angry, I could have hit him! Instead, I turned and punched the hallway door, putting my fist through it. I was left with a broken door, a hurt hand, and a shattered heart.

I was devastated by my actions. I was angry at my father for being abusive, yet here I was acting just like him.

I instantly felt like God could never use me again since I was capable of this behavior. I cried for hours. I felt hopeless and ashamed. I felt the weeds of rage and hatred choking me to death. I knew the time had come to get to the root and deal with the issue once and for all!

I cried out to God for help. I begged the Holy Spirit to help me break free of hate, anger, and rage in my life. I asked Him to set me free from the abuse that was dominating me. He answered by telling me that He was waiting for me to ask, and He would love to do this work inside of me. However, I had to allow Him to expose the hidden pain in my heart.

I was so desperate to be different that I did what I had avoided doing for over twenty years—I faced the pain of abuse inside of my heart, faced the anger, hate, and unforgiveness I had for my dad for causing me the pain, and choose to once and for all forgive him.

Now, I am not going to lie to you and tell you it was a breeze. It

HURT!

The Holy Spirit reminded me of instances in my life that I had blocked out in my mind and buried, painful times I never wanted to admit happened, worse yet, face. I had to remember - the words, the fists, the pain, the excruciating sense of rejection and pain, and the mind control and brainwashing I had experienced.

It was hard, I cried a lot of tears, and I hurt. But you know what? I also was set free and became a different man!

God slowly made me into a new man. He healed my shattered relationship with my mom. I came to find out she had no clue how my dad was isolating me from her. In time, we developed a strong healthy relationship.

I spent years in counseling. I spent hours upon hours on my face before God, seeking His will and repenting of sins in my life. I devoured the Bible, allowing it to convict me and change me. I read everything I could get my hands on about what it meant to be a man of God, a real man of God.

I will always be grateful to God for making me go through this difficult season. He restored me and my mom. God formed me into a new man. He made me usable. He helped me overcome my anger (we'll discuss this more in the next chapter), and then He began opening doors for me to share my testimony with other men.

I began writing articles for the Assemblies of God National Men's Ministry's website and for other men's ministries. I knew how God had changed my life. I experienced the freedom only He can give, and my heart's passion was to help other men experience the same freedom.

My sister Adessa often tells people that God can change anyone; she has seen it in my life. She tells them about how abusive I was, and if God hadn't set me free and made me into a new man, we never would be able to minister together like we do now. She was too afraid of me and never would have been willing to be alone with me. But God changed me and made me into a new man. He can do the same for you.

So how can you break the chains of abuse and conquer this mountain?

1. Break the Silence

I know this is tricky. You're always afraid that people won't believe you or that the person who is abusing you will get angry and punish you. You don't want to be the one to "muddy the waters" because then you'll have to deal with the consequences. Trust me, I know.

Talking breaks the cycle of secrets and secrets are the ropes that hold abusive relationships together.

Talking breaks the cycle of secrets, and secrets are the ropes that hold abusive relationships together.

You cannot break free from abuse if you allow yourself to stay alienated and alone. Instead, find trusted individuals who can help you overcome not just the abuse but the twisted thinking in your mind that wants to accept abuse. Pray for a safe person to talk to. God can bring that person to you or impress it upon you who you can trust.

2. Get Some Help

Although breaking the silence about abuse is important, it is really only the beginning of the journey. The next step is to seek the help of a godly, Christian counselor who is trained in helping people overcome the issues in their hearts and minds that caused them to accept abuse.

In an abuse situation, although it is not the victim's fault, if the victim wants to stop being victimized, they need to get some help to break the cycles of abuse and ensure that they do not become the victim again. For our family, breaking this cycle included dealing honestly with the issues of our past, (including my parents' past), seeking counseling, and even going through spiritual deliverance sessions with a trained minister.

It didn't happen overnight. We gained ground little by little as we persevered through the memories, did a lot of talking, chose to apply forgiveness, and learned new ways of thinking and living. Yet, with each counseling session we gained more ground and experienced more freedom leading to healthier lives.

3. Deal with the Conditioning

Did you know that you can crave abuse like an alcoholic craves alcohol?

If you were abused as a child or raised in an abusive household, then abuse is normal to you. You will feel safe and loved in abusive situations and you are conditioned to accept abuse. This training is something that you will need to be delivered from and work on overcoming.

Did you know that there is a generational aspect to abuse?

For many, once you've experienced abuse, there's a natural tendency to either abuse or accept abuse. I know I ended up being abusive because hurting people hurt people. That's why it's so important that each of us chooses to break the cycle and addiction to abuse in our own lives.

The truth is that if great-grandpa, grandpa, and dad accepted abuse or were abusers, then there is a high probability that you too will be prone to follow in their footsteps. In fact, most of the time, people who abuse have experienced abuse themselves. It could be from a parent, a teacher, a neighbor, a friend....really anyone.

Part of my journey to overcoming abuse meant recognizing that abuse was a generational learned behavior in our family. Left unaddressed, it would continue to go on and on. I had to break free of Mt. Abuse so I could stop being an abuser and start being a loving, godly man. I did it, and so can you.

So how do you start?

1. Soak Your Mind in God's Word and Your Heart in Prayer

Anyone who has lived through abuse knows that there's more to it than just the physical pain. That's only a small part. The real beatings come to your mind, soul, and spirit. That's why you're willing to accept the physical pain---you're already beaten down in every other area.

That's why it's so important that your road to recovery includes soaking your mind in God's Word on a daily basis and allowing the truth, light, and healing in the Word to heal your heart and reveal your true value as God's son.   As you read the Bible, it will renew your mind, shining God's light into the twisted thinking and speaking truth into the dark areas of your soul.

I remember my Mom saying that one of the things that helped her on her journey to freedom from abuse was memorizing Scripture.   A few of the Scriptures that helped her were:

> *Listen to me, O house of Jacob, all you who remain of the house of Israel, you whom I have upheld since you were conceived, and have carried since your birth. Even to your old age and gray hairs I am He, I am He who will sustain you. I have made you and I will carry you; I will sustain you and I will rescue you.*
> *-Isaiah 46:3-4 (NIV)*

> *Can a mother forget the baby at her breast and have no compassion on the child she has borne? Though she may forget, I will not forget you! See, I have engraved you on the palms of my hands; your walls are ever before me. -Isaiah 49:15-16 (NIV)*

> *Do not be afraid; you will not suffer shame. Do not fear disgrace; you will not be humiliated.   You will forget the shame of your youth and remember no more the reproach of your widowhood. For your Maker is your husband— the LORD Almighty is his name— the Holy One of Israel is your Redeemer; He is called the God of all the earth.   The LORD will call you back as if you were a wife deserted and distressed in spirit— a wife who married*

young, only to be rejected,' says your God.   -Isaiah 54:4-6 (NIV)

The Spirit of the Sovereign LORD is on me, because the LORD has anointed me to preach good news to the poor. He has sent me to bind up the brokenhearted, to proclaim freedom for the captives and release from darkness for the prisoners, to proclaim the year of the LORD's favor and the day of vengeance of our God, to comfort all who mourn, and provide for those who grieve in Zion— to bestow on them a crown of beauty instead of ashes, the oil of gladness instead of mourning, and a garment of praise instead of a spirit of despair. They will be called oaks of righteousness, a planting of the LORD for the display of his splendor. They will rebuild the ancient ruins and restore the places long devastated; they will renew the ruined cities that have been devastated for generations. -Isaiah 61:1-4 (NIV)

It's only as we begin to see ourselves through the eyes of our Heavenly Father and find our identity in Him that we begin to understand that we don't deserve to be abused. Even though your abuser may have told you you're worthless, no good, and deserve everything you get, it is a lie.

The only way to get these lies out of your brain is to flood your mind with the truth of God's Word.

Read it. Meditate on it. Listen to it as you're falling asleep at night.

As we begin to see ourselves through the eyes of our Heavenly Father and find our identity in Him, we begin to understand we don't deserve to be abused.

Focus on Scriptures that tell you how God feels about you and how much He loves you so that you can overcome the lies of your abuser.

I know it sounds like an easy answer—almost too easy---but it really is the best way to overcome abuse.

2. Forgive Your Abuser

I know it sounds absolutely impossible---almost ludicrous---but one lesson that we've learned is that one of the keys to overcoming abuse is choosing to forgive every person that ever abused you in the past.

This doesn't mean that you are saying what they did to you was right. Instead, when you forgive those who abused you, you're releasing yourself from all the anger, hate, and feelings of revenge that you are carrying toward them.

As long as you hold on to these feelings, they are still controlling you and hurting you. However, when you set them free and put them in God's hands, you're really breaking the chains they have on you so that you can walk in freedom.

3. Learn to Walk in Freedom

One of the biggest challenges for those who are accustomed to abuse is learning to walk in freedom. I know it was one of the biggest obstacles for my mom, my sister, and me. It's hard because over the years your brain forms a natural groove towards keeping the peace, being controlled, keeping your abuser happy, and accepting the blame when your abuser isn't happy. It's like learning to live in a cage.

Then someone opens the door and says, *"You're free."*

The truth is that it's pretty normal for your natural response to be, *"Now what?"* You might even be afraid to take those first few steps out of the cage and into the big, wide world around you.

So how do you do it?

You take one step at a time.

Each day you put one step in front of the other and take another step toward freedom, knowing that even the smallest baby steps are getting you closer to your goal.

4. Build a Support System

Another key to learning to walk in freedom is having a support system around you encouraging you to take each step forward and speaking words of life into your spirit.

For example, I was used to abusing my body. I had conquered a lot of my abusive ways, but this was an area within myself that I couldn't see as being abusive. I was trained to think I deserved to suffer. Then one day my mentor started talking to me about taking better care of myself by taking time off (I'll share more of this story in our Mt. Failure chapter), eating healthier, and getting proper sleep. He showed me that I needed to take care of myself if I was going to survive as a minister. I had to overcome my mindset of inflicting self-abuse physically to follow God wholeheartedly.

His support helped me to be a more balanced, healthier person. He helped me conquer the abuse in an area I couldn't see. Now I live better, eat healthier, and am way better at pacing my time.

Healthy thinking has replaced abuse, and I'm now living in freedom.

But it started one step at a time, choosing to step out of the cage and walk in freedom from abuse.

Today, if you're reading this and you're suffering under the terror of abuse, I hope this chapter encourages you to take your own steps out of the cage and into freedom. Whether it be admitting to yourself that you need help, breaking your silence, seeking help, or making the choice to forgive and walk in freedom, I encourage you that today is the day to start.

Don't continue being the victim of another person's unresolved issues. Instead, take personal responsibility and decide that you are going to take your own first baby steps toward freedom.

As someone who has taken the journey to freedom and overcome, I can tell you it is well worth every effort.

Maybe you're reading this and realizing that you have morphed from being abused to becoming an abuser. You need to overcome! You can't keep being abusive to others in your life. You need to take this chapter VERY seriously and start allowing God to heal you from the abuse in your past. It is the only way to stop being an abuser in the future.

Follow the steps listed in this book.

Allow the Holy Spirit to heal you from your abusive memories and to take away the pain.

Begin to forgive your abuser.

Don't ignore this call to change today!

You must climb Mt. Abuse once and for all. Victory can be yours!

Dear Heavenly Father,

I want to be free of abuse. Help me with painful memories, to overcome the pain, and to move forward, free of the abuse.

Give me the strength to break the silence of abuse. Help me to find someone who I can trust to help me work through the issues from the abuse I received in the past and any ways in which I'm now being abusive. Help me to walk in freedom, free from the big shadow of Mt. Abuse.

Father, forgive me for every time I have been an abuser. Help me to commit to leaving my abusive ways behind me and becoming a loving, kind, and gentle man. I want to be free from Mt. Abuse forever. Help me! In Jesus' name, Amen.

GROUP STUDY QUESTIONS:

1. Why is it important to break the silence to conquer abuse?

2. We said in this chapter that it is possible to become so familiar with abuse that you can actually crave it. Why do you think this is, and what does it mean to you?

3. Why is it important to understand how God feels about you to conquer abuse?

4. Who can be your support system to help you defeat abuse in your life?

5. After reading this chapter, what is one thing you will put into practice or one thing you will change in your life?

6. How can we, as a group, help you do this?

-Chapter Five-

Mt. Anger

"Now would be a really good time to get angry."

"Cap, that's my secret, I'm always angry."[1]

These famous lines from *The Avengers* are great if you're a superhero battling an enemy, but for a man of God, they are a huge roadblock keeping us from becoming all God wants us to be.

One of the biggest mountains that men are struggling to conquer today is Mt. Anger. It actually ranks higher than pornography.

Does this surprise you? It did me, but when you stop and really think about it, it is true. How often does cable news report stories of men murdering their wives or girlfriends?

Murder is the extreme end of rage. More common are beatings, abuse, verbal abuse, screaming fits, tantrums, and many other manifestations that destroy our relationships.

Men are having fits of anger and rage around the world, resulting in abuse, scars, broken marriages, broken families, and broken relationships.

We need to stop living at the foot of Mt. Anger. If we are to be men of God, we need to get to the root of our anger and yank it out once and for all. Only then can we live free of our anger and rage and become calm, compassionate, loving men of God.

So what is the root of anger?

The root of almost all anger, hate, and rage is unforgiveness.

Someone in your life did something to you, and it hurt you and caused you pain. Instead of facing the pain, dealing with it, and forgiving the person who hurt you, many of us deny the pain, deny the action that hurt us, and we ignore the pain. We bury the pain inside of our hearts.

However, because the issue was just buried and not dealt with, it takes root in our heart, and slowly it grows, blossoming into anger, hatred, and rage. Instead of dealing with the pain, we become a hateful, cruel person who pops at the slightest injury. Afterward, we are left devastated and alone, wondering why we just inflicted pain on the ones we love.

It's like the story I told you in the last chapter about the night I punched the door. Because I had never dealt with the anger I felt towards my dad for his abuse, I ended up exploding in anger myself.

Guys, it is time for God's men to stop living in this childish behavior and start conquering Mt. Anger! We can do this by once and for all facing the unforgiveness, hate, and pain in our lives and allowing the Holy Spirit to heal us.

"But Jamie, didn't we just discuss this in the last chapter on abuse?"

Yes and no. Some of the principles overlap as you saw when I shared my testimony. While every man who is abusive is angry, not every man who is angry becomes abusive.

I have found that most abusive anger and rage starts as hatred. This is not a new thing. Ever since Cain's hatred led him to murder his brother Abel, anger and rage have been an issue for men. It was apparently an issue for the believers in the early church, because one of my favorite men in the Bible, John, wrote about it in his epistle to the early church.

> *Dear friends, I am not writing you a new command but an old one, which you have had since the beginning. This old command is the message you have heard. Yet I am writing you a new command; its truth is seen in him and in you, because the darkness is passing and the true light is already shining. -1 John 2:7-8 (NIV)*

John gets his reader's attention by introducing his topic in a way that grabs their interest. He says he has a new commandment for them, but in reality, it is an old commandment. Logically, the reader would be glued to the text, trying to see where he is going with this. John doesn't keep them in suspense long as he immediately lays out what he wants them to know.

> *Anyone who claims to live in God's light and hates a brother or sister is still in the dark. It's the person who loves brother and sister who dwells in God's light and doesn't block the light from others. But whoever hates is still in the dark, stumbles around in the dark, doesn't know which end is up, blinded by the darkness. - 1 John 2:8-11 (The Message)*

Ouch! John hits them right between the eyes. He puts it quite bluntly. If you hate someone, you're not walking under the influence of God. You're instead following the ways of the enemy and his dark kingdom.

John puts it quite bluntly, if you hate someone, you're not walking under the influence of God.

John remembered Jesus' commands to love one another and to live in unity with all people. He remembered Jesus' teaching that we need to love our enemies and to do good to those who despitefully use them. He saw Jesus set the example by turning the other cheek. THAT is walking in the light.

Hating someone or holding unforgiveness against them doesn't line up with what John learned from Jesus, so he tells them quite bluntly, *"If you're harboring hate, if you're not forgiving, if you're consumed by anger, you're not truly following God."*

Sound too harsh? Does it ruffle feathers to say it so bluntly? Good! That was exactly what John was hoping to do! He wanted his readers to realize the seriousness of allowing hate and anger into their lives. It was important to him that they would see the downward spiral. What is this spiral?

1. Unforgiveness Leads to Hate

When we forgive someone, we extend to them the same mercy and grace that God extended to us when we repented and accepted Him as our Lord and Savior. When we refuse to forgive, we pull mercy and grace away and instead replace it with hate, revenge, and a host of other ungodly behaviors.

2. Hate Leads to Anger

Hate is a lot like mold. It starts small, but spreads quickly, and eventually consumes everything that it comes in contact with it.

Not only that, but it destroys the things it connects itself to.

The same is true when hate takes root in our lives. We start out hating one person, but then the hatred spreads to our other relationships. We become an angry, bitter person, and as a result, we end up destroying our relationships with others. Bruce Banner's words, *"You won't like me when I get angry,"* become the motto we live by. We become angry people who lash out at others to hurt them instead of being loving people who reach out to others to help them.

3. Anger Turns to Rage

Unresolved anger doesn't just stay inside of us. We may try to suppress it, but it eventually comes out. Like the Hulk who comes out of Bruce Banner, our pent up anger that is never dealt with quickly morphs into rage and that's when we have violent outbreaks and episodes.

If I had a nickel for all the men who told me they have punched doors or walls out of rage, I'd be quite comfortable. This doesn't even include the men who let out their rage on wives and kids instead of walls and doors. Their behavior then starts a new cycle of anger and hate in a new generation. And on and on it goes...it must STOP!

John got this and wrote to the people that, if you hate someone, your Christianity is in trouble. Today I say the same thing to you. If you're harboring hate, you're spiritual in trouble.

If you're letting anger consume you and your relationships, you're in spiritual trouble.

If you're hitting your wife and kids, I'll go so far as to say you're in deep spiritual trouble...you need to turn to God and repent and start again.

Abusing your wife and kids goes against many of the fruits of the Spirit (Galatians 5:22-23)

> If you're hitting your wife and kids, I'll go so far as to say you're in deep spiritual trouble...you need to turn to God and repent and start again.

The Bible is clear that if you are not treating your wife properly, God isn't hearing your prayers. (1 Peter 3:7).

Paul says to love your wife as Christ loves the church (Ephesians 5:25-29) and Christ DOES NOT abuse his church.

If you fit into this category, repent, get right with God, and GET

HELP FOR YOUR PROBLEM! Go to a counselor to deal with your issues and to deal with the ground you have given to spirits of anger, rage, abuse, hatred, and unforgiveness.

Yes, I know this is a lot tougher and blunter than any we have had before, but I feel a burning passion from the Holy Spirit to write these words. If your hate, anger, and rage have gotten out of control, ask God for forgiveness and beg Him for deliverance. Seek out a counselor, face the issues, deal with the original issue that caused hate, and stop tormenting those who God has entrusted to your care. Get right with God, and change.

How do we do this?

By getting to the root cause of your anger.

• When did it start?

• Who was there with you?

• What was going on?

• How did you feel experiencing this?

• How did you respond?

You need to remember the first time you felt the anger, feel the pain, face it, and deal with it once and for all.

Maybe you are thinking, *"Jamie, I can't do this. It hurts too much, and I just don't have it inside of me to do it."*

My answer to you is that you are absolutely right! It does hurt to face the buried memories and forgive, and you don't have it in you to do it. However, you do have the Holy Spirit on your side, and He has the strength to do this work inside of you.

How do I know? Because He did it in my life.

Surprised? Many people are.

You see, when people first meet me, they describe me as funny, kind, gentle, and caring. I am the guy who plays with the church kids, hugs the hurting, and shows mercy to others when they hurt me. I don't say this braggingly, because I know I am only this way through the power of the Holy Spirit. You see, I know what I used to be.

I used to be a boiling pot! I used to be the world's moodiest man. You never knew what you would get with me. One minute I was the life of the party, the next I was withdrawn, silent, and depressed. Anger ruled my life, and it didn't take much to make my hot temper explode. I was a powder keg of anger, rage, and hate. The problem was, I didn't know why. After an explosion when I would hurt those around me, I was just as confused as to why I exploded as the people closest to me.

Even as a young adult serving God and trying to be an effective minister, I would have fits of anger and rage. Instead of digging deep into my heart and finding the root of the action, I would weed whack the sin and keep it looking neat and presentable. It looked good, and people would admire the good things surrounding the weeds in my heart, but the weeds never went away. They were still there, and they continued to grow and expose themselves from time to time. I was stuck in a awful pattern of loving and serving God, followed by outbursts of anger and rage, and then repentance and promises it would never happen again. But it just kept happening!

Then I had the experience we discussed in the last chapter where I cried out to God after I punched the door. The Holy Spirit made me face the pain, and He helped me forgive my dad.

One of the things the Holy Spirit made me do was stop looking at my dad through the childish eyes of pain and see Him through the eyes of a man. I saw how my father's actions were a result of the pain he experienced in his own life. Just like my actions and rage were results of unforgiveness and repressed issues, so were his. He experienced nightmares I couldn't imagine, and his action towards me were actually his reaction to his own heart weeds.

What God asked me to do was hard, but I knew he was right; I had to forgive my dad. I began to see that if I didn't forgive him, I would continue through life chained to this sin, and I would follow my Dad's example and pass it on to another generation.

If I wanted God to forgive me for my actions and show me compassion and mercy, then I needed to show my dad the same compassion and mercy. I had to become a forgiving man in order to climb past Mt. Anger. The same is true for everyone.

You may be thinking, *"I understand the importance of forgiveness, but I just don't feel like I can forgive this person. What can I do?"*

Let me be the first to tell you this: there is hope.

It doesn't matter if you feel like you can't forgive someone. You can't wait for this feeling to come. Forgiveness is not an emotion. It is a mental decision you need to make. You must consciously decide, *"I am going to forgive that person."* It has to be a decision you make of your own free will.

Forgiveness is not an emotion. It is a mental decision you need to make.

When God first started dealing with me about the need to forgive others, He showed me that I had to do it even if I didn't feel like it.

Daily, I had to decide to forgive my dad.

It was hard. I didn't want to forgive. Sometimes it meant saying it over and over again---sometimes twenty times a day choosing again and again---*"I am going to forgive him"* even when I didn't want to.

But that's the point---it isn't about the *"want to"*—it's a matter of obedience. We forgive because we are forgiven and God commands it.

Don't worry about feeling it---the feeling of forgiveness may take time to come. Just keep choosing to forgive because you want to be free.

I remembered my mom told me a few ways she had learned to help change her heart to forgive. I used them, and they helped. I now want to share them with you.

The first thing she told me was to begin to ask God to bless the person that you need to forgive. Jesus commanded us to bless those who despitefully use us (Matt.5:44). We need to follow this pattern. Ask God to bless the person, provide for their needs, and help them become all that He wants them to be. It is hard to feel hatred and unforgiveness while praying for the person's good.

The second thing she taught me was to do something nice for the person. This is a principle Jesus taught us in Luke 6:27. Is it always easy? No! But it will heal your soul.

Here's a personal example:

I remember a time when my dad developed a foot injury that required a clean bandage and cleansing every morning. It was on a spot of his foot where he couldn't reach to apply the bandage, so God required me to get up each day and dress his wound, all the while still receiving his criticism and nasty disposition. I did it for God and endured the treatment because I wanted to be free from any unforgiveness and anger in my heart.

This is just one example of how we need to try and find a way to do good for the person we have unforgiveness toward, even if it is as simple as buying them a cup of coffee or helping them do a home repair project. You will be able to do it. How do I know? Because Jesus did it.

If ever there was a man who had the right to harbor unforgiveness, it was Jesus.

He was beaten, almost to death. He was mocked. He was spit upon. He was ridiculed, despised, and abused. He was hung on a cross even though He was totally innocent and sinless. He had every reason in the word to hate, be angry, and seek vengeance. He had every right in the world to destroy everyone around the cross for what they did to

Him, and He had the power and ability to do it.

But He didn't! Instead, He asked His Father to forgive them! He did good to His enemies. We need to do the same.

The third thing she taught me was that you need to forgive the person; however, you can't condone their evil behavior. Forgiveness doesn't mean you allow the person to keep sinning against you.

I have, through the power of the Holy Spirit, forgiven my dad, but I do not allow him to abuse me either. My forgiveness is not a license for him to be abusive. When he acts abusively, I lovingly confront him and let him know it is unacceptable and WILL NOT continue. However, I make sure hatred, anger, or unforgiveness doesn't grow inside of me either.

True forgiveness allows you to take a stand against the evil behavior while not allowing anger, bitterness and hate to consume you. Forgiveness is really as much for your own mental and spiritual condition as it is for the other person. It is the key to overcoming Mt. Anger.

We must all decide today that we will no longer stay at the foot of Mt. Anger. Instead, we choose to conquer Mt. Anger and forgive.

There is no room for anger or hatred among God's men. We can't let it destroy our lives, our families, and our relationships any longer. We can't continue dragging God and Christianity through the mud as we claim to be a Christian, but live like someone in darkness. We can't allow it to separate us from God and becoming everything He wants us to be.

So I encourage you, no I beg you, to take this chapter seriously! Take immediate action. Do not delay.

Dear Heavenly Father,

You know my struggle with anger in my life. Father, I no longer want anger to consume my life; I want to conquer Mt. Anger!

Father, forgive me for every time I have been an angry, out-of-control man. Show me the cause of my anger. Help me to forgive the person who hurt me. Forgive me for burying my feelings of unforgiveness, anger, and hatred. Help me to truly forgive.

Make me into a kind, gentle, loving man of God. Help me, once and for all, defeat the anger inside of me. In Jesus' name, Amen.

GROUP STUDY QUESTIONS:

1. We said that most abusive anger starts as hatred. What are your thoughts on this?

2. Why does hate cause separation between us and God?

3. Discuss this statement: *"If you're hitting your wife and kids, I'll go so far as to say you're beyond being in spiritual trouble...you need to turn to God and repent and start again."*

4. What is something nice you can do for the person you need to forgive?

5. After reading this chapter, what is one thing you will put into practice or one thing you will change in your life?

6. How can we, as a group, help you do this?

–Chapter Six–

Mt. Shame

Have you ever seen a little kid who sees another kid doing something wrong? Many times this child will rub their two index fingers together and say, "Shame, shame!"

Being a big softy for kids, I always find this so cute. We see nothing wrong with this action. It doesn't scar the child, and sometimes it helps them realize they are doing something wrong.

It's quite a different story when you're older. Shame can cripple you as an adult. Why else do you think the enemy tries to use shame to keep us sidelined? He uses shame to keep us from entering into our Promised Land.

Shame can be devastating! It makes us think thoughts like:

• I am not good enough for God's blessing.

• I can't overcome…You have no idea what I have done.

• How could God ever forgive me?

• I've made too much of a mess of things.

• I can't forgive myself.

On and on goes the list of the ways shame lies to us to keep us stuck at the foot of its mountain, keeping us from rising up and becoming what God calls us to be.

Shame has been a HUGE mountain in my life. Next to fear, it is probably the second biggest mountain I've had to climb.

In the previous chapters, we looked at my story of overcoming my dad's abuse, and in the last chapter we discussed my issues with how abuse and unforgiveness caused me to be an angry young man. In this chapter, we are going to look at the results of my anger issues, and the shame I battle because of them.

You see, I was not always a kind person. (I know, you're so shocked you had to pick up the book after dropping it!) But seriously, a lot of people know who I am now, who God shaped me into, but few know who I used to be, and who I used to be is shameful to me.

My dad was very abusive to our entire family. Like many abusers, one of the tactics he employed to keep his behavior a secret was doing everything he could to keep my mom and me separated. As awful and painful as this is to write, my dad's lies to me about my mom and her feelings toward me caused me to be a horrible son to my mom during my late childhood and teenage years.

The basic issue was that my dad lied to me about my mom (while at the same time lying to her about me.) He painted a picture of her that simply wasn't true, blaming everything that was wrong in our lives on her deep passion and devotion to Jesus and her commitment to following Biblical principles. *"If your mom wasn't such a religious fanatic, we could have that, or do that, or go there...."* were his go-to lines.

Looking back now, I can see that these lies were to cover up his secrets, his lies, and his lack of responsibility and accountability with life and relationships, but as a child, I believed what he said. As a young man, these lies caused me to resent my mom's rules and believe that she'd taken this Jesus thing just a little too far.

Eventually, I rebelled and chose a more casual Christian lifestyle.

Whenever my mom would confront me about the sin in my life, I'd fight with her and punish her for telling me I was wrong. This pattern continued until the Holy Spirit woke me up and made me realize she was right and I needed to change. Yet, even after I changed, my bad behavior toward her became a great source of shame.

Of course, painting my Mom as a Jesus Freak was only a small part of my dad's lies. The much greater, more devastating lie that he told me was that my mom didn't love me or want me. Looking back as an adult, I can see that this was textbook abusive behavior, but, as a child, it filled me with questions, pain, and fear. I felt isolated. Like many abused children, I turned my anger and pain toward the parent who could have helped (had she known) and idolized my dad.

I was so twisted. My dad was my abuser, yet I idolized him. My mom was the "good parent," the one who loved and protected me, the one who cared about me and how I turned out in life. Yet, she received my anger and abusive treatment, not my dad.

The result was that I turned into an angry, rebellious, smart-mouthed kid who constantly went to battle with my mom. I would argue with her and fight her on everything. I was a very moody child and teen. I could set the tone of an entire room, and often these moods were directed at my mom. I was a selfish and spoiled child who made life very hard for my mom. I insisted on having the newest and best of everything, whether we could afford it or not.

I was just so angry. I had no idea that my dad was abusing my mom, lying to my mom about me, or that the way my dad was treating me was wrong. It's very hard for me to remember the fights, the way I emotionally and verbally abused my mom, or even the way I thought back then. Even though I now understand "why" it happened, I still truly wish it had never been this way.

Thankfully, the Holy Spirit intervened and changed me when I was in my early twenties. The night I punched the door, I broke, and finally allowed God to work on my heart. As he showed me the abuse and pain that I had repressed, I could finally begin to see the truth.

Over the next few months as we went through counseling, my dad's secret abuse was revealed to both my mom and me. It was shocking for both of us to learn how my dad had manipulated both of us to keep us apart. She had no idea I was being abused, and Adessa and I had no idea about the abuse that she was tolerating behind closed doors. We were both brokenhearted that so many years of our lives were stolen from us because we trusted someone we loved.

During this time, my mom and I spent a lot of time talking. We asked each other for forgiveness for the things we didn't know and the lies we'd believed. As our entire family went through counseling and spiritual deliverance, we were able to see that we were both victims who were kept away from the other so that the truth wasn't exposed.

God began to change me into a new man, and slowly my mom and I were able to develop a relationship. God restored us, and we became very close and had a great relationship. I am so grateful to God for the years He gave us together and the relationship He developed between us.

Then, unexpectedly, my mom passed away. While I was grateful for the years we had together and the relationship we developed, shame really attacked me.

- Why did I treat her that way?

- Why didn't I help her deal with my dad's abuse instead of making things even more difficult?

- Why couldn't I have let stuff go and caused her less grief and stress?

- Why didn't I spend more time with her?

- Why did I have to make life so hard on her?

This is a huge source of shame in my life. At times, it can be crippling. The shame and regret of my behavior is a struggle I still battle to this day. I still often have nightmares where I am arguing and fighting with my mom, and I wake up feeling so sad and ashamed of how I used to treat her.

I know I am not the same man anymore. I know God set me free and completely changed me. I know my mom saw this change. I know for 5 years or more of my life, my mom was my mentor who helped train me and make me into the man I am now. But I still struggle with feelings of shame for what I was and how I treated her. If I could have one thing in life, it would be to have my mom tell me she is proud of the man I have become and the ministry I am doing. (Because unfortunately, she passed away before God opened doors of ministry.)

Why am I sharing all of this? Because I want you to see that I get how huge of a mountain shame can be. I get the crippling obstacle it is in our walk with God. I know how it feels to regret something so much and have it be such a great source of shame in your life. But I also know shame can be conquered, and freedom can come!

Honestly, one of the reasons I think I have so many nightmares about this is because the enemy knows he can't get to me anymore while I am awake, so he hits me when I'm asleep. Victory is possible. Mt. Shame can be climbed! First, we need to learn more about shame and then we'll look at ways to overcome.

Shame Comes In All Shapes and Sizes

I recently heard shame defined as "*a sense deep inside that there is something fundamentally wrong with you.*"

The Free Dictionary defines it as a painful emotion caused by a sense of guilt, embarrassment, unworthiness, or disgrace.

It can be a mix of regret, self-hate, and dishonor. Those describe exactly how I felt in the stories above.

Dr. Kristalyn Salters-Pedneault defines shame as, "*An emotion in which the self is perceived as defective, unacceptable, or fundamentally damaged. Shame is often confused with guilt, which is related but distinct emotion in which a specific behavior is viewed as unacceptable or wrong, rather than the entire self. People who experience traumatic events are prone to shame, particularly if they blame themselves for the event. Shame can be a particularly problematic emotion because it is associated with a desire to hide, disappear, or even die."[1]*

Here's the thing I've learned about shame: Often we associate these things with "big sins." We tend to think that only people who've lived a really bad, sinful life understand what shame feels like.

We define shame as feeling regret for things we've done.

But what I've learned about shame is that it comes in all shapes and sizes and clings to people of all backgrounds and cultures. The truth is that the church member who has spent every week of their life inside the church can be struggling with just as much shame and insecurity as a person with a colorful past.

- Some feel shame because of their weight or their appearance.

- Others experience shame because of their lack of education or job experience.

- Many experience shame because of their past or their family background.

The problem with shame is that it doesn't focus on any one demographic, but rather, it tries to attack at every economic, social, and age level pointing out either insufficiencies, insecurities, or the mistakes made in the past. Its goal is to cause you to be so overcome by the things you aren't or the things you've done that you become a prisoner.

Shame wants to control you.

It wants to make you hide away and never become the strong, godly, competent person that God created you to be.

That's really why our enemy uses this weapon on so many Christians. He's afraid of what they could become if they allowed Jesus to control their life rather than shame. He's afraid of the life they'd live, the people they'd influence, and the difference they could make among their family, their friends, their community, and ultimately for the kingdom of God.

The best way he knows of to stop us is to attack us with shame. If he can make us feel unworthy, unloved, unwanted, and unnecessary, there's always the chance that we'll agree with him and say, *"You know what, that's right, I can't do what God wants me to do. I can't live the way God wants me to live and be who God's called me to be. Why am I even trying?"*

It's one of the enemy's top plays in his centuries-old playbook. However, thanks to Jesus, we can recognize this strategy and overcome it, throwing off the chains of shame, once and for all, and walking in the freedom of Jesus Christ.

How Do We Overcome Shame?

1. We Need to Recognize Shame For What It Is: An Attack of the Enemy Who Wants to Destroy Us.

The first step in winning any battle is recognizing that you are at war.

When you are constantly being barraged with bombshells from an enemy, you are under attack. When you decide to fight back---you are at war.

> When you are constantly being barraged with bombshells from an enemy, you are under attack. When you decide to fight back---you are at war.

For too long, Christians have allowed the enemy to constantly attack them with the lies of shame telling them they aren't good enough, they can never accomplish anything, they aren't worthy of God's love, and they have no potential.

Because they are unwilling to fight the battle spiritually, lives are being destroyed and devastated by the enemy's terrorism.

However, this does not have to continue.

As God's sons, we can recognize that we are in a spiritual battle and choose to use the spiritual weapons that God has given us to fight against the lies of the enemy.

The first step toward this end is standing up and saying, *"I recognize that this is a spiritual attack. The enemy wants to destroy me, but I'm not going to let him. Instead, I'm going to use the Sword of the Word of God to fight these lies and gain the victory."*

This is what I do on the mornings I wake up after the nightmares.

2. Use the Bible to Recognize Your True Identity as God's Child.

Shame tells you all of the things that you are not. However, the truth of the Bible wants to tell you who you are: First and foremost, you are God's chosen child, holy and loved.

> *What marvelous love the Father has extended to us! Just look at it—we're called children of God! That's who we really are.* - *I John 1:31 (The Message)*

> *Praise be to the God and Father of our Lord Jesus Christ, who has blessed us in the heavenly realms with every spiritual blessing in Christ. For he chose us in him before the creation of the world to be holy and blameless in his sight. In love he predestined us for adoption to sonship through Jesus Christ, in accordance with his pleasure and will——— In him we were also chosen, having been predestined according to the plan of him who works out everything in conformity with the purpose of his will.* - *Ephesians 1:3-5,11 (NIV)*

Because God chose us and adopted us, we are literally now sons of the King of the Universe. Even before you knew Him, God chose you. He reached out to you. He made a way through His Son Jesus Christ for you to be adopted and become His child.

3. Insert Truth: God Didn't Choose You Because of the Things You Could or Couldn't Do.

God was never interested in the lists of what you are or what you're not. He didn't choose you because of your abilities, your appearance, your education, your financial status, or your relationship status.

> *Take a good look, friends, at who you were when you got called into this life. I don't see many of "the brightest and the best" among you, not many influential, not many from high-society families. Isn't it obvious that God deliberately chose men and women that the culture overlooks and exploits and abuses, chose these "nobodies" to expose the hollow pretensions of the "somebodies"? -1 Corinthians 1:26-28 (The Message)*

So what is the antidote to the lies of the enemy when shame wants to list all the ways in which you are not good enough?

Well, it's to agree with a twist.

The twist is that God doesn't care.

Even before you knew Him, God chose you and made a way through His Son Jesus for you to be adopted and become His. And even knowing all of your faults and flaws, shortcomings and weaknesses, He still chose you and said, *"I know what you are not. But if you will surrender yourself to me and let me mold you into the*

Even knowing all of your faults and flaws, shortcomings and weaknesses, God still chose you!

image of my Son, Jesus Christ. If you will obey me and follow the path I've laid out for your life---I am going to do amazing things with your life. Things that NOBODY could imagine. I'm not only going to revolutionize your life, but I'm going to use them to start a revolution in my kingdom."

By ourselves we really are nothing, but Jesus specializes in taking nothing and using it to bring glory to Himself.

That's why one of the best ways to fight an attack of Shame is to come back with: *"I may not be all of the things you are listing, but God doesn't care. He still chose me to be His child, and He still has a plan to fulfill in my life."*

4. Getting to the Root of the Problem

Whenever an enemy declares war, they always start by finding areas that are the most vulnerable to attack---the weaknesses. One thing I've learned in my own life is that in my battle with Mt. Shame, Satan always attacks in my weakest areas—where I'm most vulnerable.

That's why one of the keys to conquering Mt. Shame in our lives is getting to the root of the problem, dealing with it and shoring up the weak areas.

For instance, in my own effort to overcome shame in my life, I've had to face the parts of my past that created vulnerable areas in my soul and mind.

The only way I could overcome my issues with shame was to face my past, forgive my dad, and I had to forgive myself. Then I had to remind myself that, yes, I hurt my mom and our relationship, but the bad dreams and memories were from the distant past. In the more recent past, my mom and I had restored our relationship. Years of my life revolved around taking care of my mom and protecting her. I gave up my entire life to do this. Yes, I had been a really bad son in the past, but God had also made me into a really good son, too. These terrible dreams and memories were not the finale to the story. Things had changed and were different.

That's why I encourage you---if you're struggling with shame, allow the Holy Spirit to heal the root of the problem in your life.

If you need to go to a counselor to deal with your issues, then do it.

Don't allow shame to control you. Instead, take control of it by going to the root and tearing it out, saying, *"You're not going to control my life any longer. I will be free!"*

5. Accept God's Forgiveness and New Life

Another big weapon that the enemy uses to attack God's people with shame is by reminding them of the sins of their past. Instead of reminding you of what you are not, he reminds you of what you were, with lies like:

• "There's no way you can serve God with your history."

• "How do you ever expect to be used by God after what you've done or after what you've lived through?"

• "You're never going to overcome this area of your life. It's going to haunt you and plague you for the rest of your life---you'll never be free. You might as well just give up now."

Again, the goal is to get you to stop moving ahead with God's plan for your life, which is to keep moving forward in obedience, and instead wallow in the chains of your past.

Once again, the key to overcoming is recognizing that this is a lie and choosing to fight shame with the truth of God's Word.

> *2 Corinthians 5:17 says, "Therefore, if anyone is in Christ, the new creation has come: The old has gone, the new is here!" (NIV)*

> *Isaiah 43:18-19 says "Forget about what's happened; don't keep going over old history. Be alert, be present. I'm about to do something brand-new. It's bursting out! Don't you see it? There it is! I'm making a road through the desert, rivers in the badlands" (The Message)*

Look at this truth from Romans 8:31-35:

> *So, what do you think? With God on our side like this, how can we lose? If God didn't hesitate to put everything on the line for us, embracing our condition and exposing himself to the worst by*

83

sending his own Son, is there anything else he wouldn't gladly and freely do for us? And who would dare tangle with God by messing with one of God's chosen? Who would dare even to point a finger? The One who died for us—who was raised to life for us!—is in the presence of God at this very moment sticking up for us. Do you think anyone is going to be able to drive a wedge between us and Christ's love for us? There is no way! Not trouble, not hard times, not hatred, not hunger, not homelessness, not bullying threats, not backstabbing, not even the worst sins listed in Scripture. (The Message)

No matter what happened in your past, you are not living there anymore. If you have repented and are wholeheartedly following Jesus and allowing Him to shape you into His image, then in God's eyes, the past is forgotten. When He looks at you now, He sees the blood of Jesus paid at Calvary. That's what it means to be justified; in God's eyes it is just as if you have never sinned.

Because of this fact, Satan has no right to use the weapon of shame against you. You are a new creation, living a new life. That may have been who you were...but it is not who you are now. If you want to overcome shame, you need to accept Christ's forgiveness, forgive

Satan has no right to use the weapon of Shame against you. You are a new creation, living a new life.

yourself for the past, and claim your new identity as God's child, living your life for His glory.

6. If You Really Want To Defeat Shame Once and For All, Share Your Testimony.

The Apostle Paul is one of my favorite men in the Bible. Why? Because he never forgot where he came from and all that God had delivered him from. Dude had a lot to be ashamed of!

Paul's past was a past of arrogance, pride, hatred, anger, and murder. He was so sure of his brilliance in understanding religion that he went on a jihad to kill all the Christians who were no longer following the Jewish religious customs. He totally missed the Jesus movement in his time. Instead of realizing a move of God was taking place, he went against it and tried to destroy it.

He literally attacked, arrested, and killed God's children. How's that for a shameful past! But then he encountered God face-to-face, and his life was never the same.

Paul could have allowed the disgrace of his past actions to keep him trapped at the foot of Mt. Shame, but instead he used his disgrace to reach more people. He used his shame-filled testimony to reach the lost and show them how powerful God is and how anyone could be forgiven of anything they did in their lives.

Over the years fighting my own battle with shame, one thing I've learned is that whenever I choose to share the testimony of what Christ has done in my life, whenever I allow Christ to take the weak areas of my life and use them for His glory, shame has to run and hide.

Why?

Because all of shame's power is lost when you decide to come out of hiding, tell the truth, admit your areas of weakness and say, *"Let the parts of my life that Satan wants to use to fill me with shame and use to devour me and my future, become a testimony of your faithfulness, of your mercy, of your power to intervene and bring life and freedom. God, if you can do anything with the ashes of my life, then feel free to make them beautiful."*

As I shared with you, all of the years of me being an abusive, angry, hurting boy and man caused me a lot of shame. Thankfully, the story doesn't end there. Instead, the story continued as God healed the broken areas of my life and helped me find my true identity and purpose in Him.

I hope this chapter inspires you to believe that shame can be overcome! Whatever its source, whatever role it's playing in your life, if you apply these steps to your own life, the Holy Spirit will be faithful and will deliver you from shame if you will cooperate with Him and fight.

You can conquer Mt Shame. Freedom from shame is possible. I encourage you to start taking steps in that direction today.

Dear Heavenly Father,

I am tired of being crippled by shame in my life. I feel so unworthy and so inadequate to feel Your love and move forward to where You have called me to go. I don't feel I will ever be good enough to be called Your son.

Father, please help me conquer Mt. Shame. Help me fight this mental battle. Help me come to the place where I realize You do love me, do want me, and do forgive me. Help me get to the root of my shame so I can overcome.

In Jesus' name, Amen.

GROUP STUDY QUESTIONS:

1. We said that *"shame is a sense deep inside that there is something fundamentally wrong with you."* How would you define shame?

2. Why is important to understand that shame is an attack from the enemy?

3. Why is knowing and memorizing verses of how God sees you important to conquering shame?

4. Why is it important to get to the root cause of our shame?

5. How does sharing your testimony help defeat shame?

6. After reading this chapter, what is one thing you will put into practice or one thing you will change in your life?

7. How can we, as a group, help you do this?

–CHAPTER SEVEN–

MT. FAILURE

Failure should be our teacher, not our undertaker. Failure is delay, not defeat. It is a temporary detour, not a dead end. - Denis Waitley[1]

I love this quote. But I would add one thing to it:

Failure should not stop us; it should motivate us to climb.

Unfortunately, too many people let their failures stop them dead in their tracks. Too scared of failing again, they make camp at the foot of Mt. Failure. They settle in and get comfortable, unwilling to risk another attempt at the climb.

I am no stranger to failure. I mentioned earlier that, after I graduated college, I came home to live with my parents. No ministry positions opened up for me after graduation, so I was forced to move home. Now, in today's culture, this is a normal, everyday occurrence. However, twenty years ago, it just wasn't done.

Yes, God's perfect will for me was to move home and deal once and for all with all the garbage polluting my soul. So in God's eyes, I wasn't a failure. But in the eyes of friends, relatives, neighbors, myself, and pretty much everyone else, I was a huge, complete and utter failure.

Some people rejoiced in seeing me fail. They enjoyed seeing the "perfect Holden family" (what a joke) not be perfect. Others pitied me. No matter the reaction, the sentiment was universal. I was a failure who couldn't get a job and who had to live off of his parents.

Like Hester Prinn wore her Scarlett "A," I carried the stigma of a failure and was filled with shame for over ten years. To all around, I was a huge failure.

My failure led to depression. I was soon stuck in idleness, unable to move forward.

Eventually, God allowed me to minister. While everyone around was stunned by this, no one was more stunned than me. Even though ministry doors opened, I still lived in the world of failure.

I remember the first time I saw my Bible college mentor after I went into ministry. The first time he saw me he cried (and every time after that!) because he never thought I would be able to minister after failing so miserably!

You see, I knew I had failed. I felt I had to prove to everyone and everything that I was as good as they were. For the first few years of ministry, I would work sixty to seventy hours a week. I never took days off. I was so stuck at the base of Mt. Failure that I was literally killing myself trying to prove I wasn't a failure.

You may think I am exaggerating. But I am not.

I felt to take a day off was showing I couldn't keep up or that I wasn't as good as everyone else. Eventually my coach/mentor stopped me and said, *"You need to stop this behavior. God called you to minister, and if you don't start taking time off or working less, you're going to burn out. You'll fizzle out after a few years. I don't want that for you. I want you to finish the marathon!"*

He was right, as much as I hated to hear it. I went home and started talking to God about why I was pushing myself so hard, and

He showed me that I was still seeing myself as a failure. I was trying to prove myself to others.

God started to show me it was time to climb Mt. Failure. I had to realize that, yes, I had failed in the past. Yes, I had made mistakes. But God hadn't left me because of my failure. He used it to make me into who He wanted me to be.

Now my job is to help others experience this same freedom. As Winston Churchill once said, *"Success is not final, failure is not fatal: it is the courage to continue that counts."*[2]

You see, failure is not an end, it's a detour.

Okay, my plans didn't turn out the way I wanted. But it wasn't the end of my life. It was just a detour. The same is true for you and your failures. They don't have to define you. You can get back up and start again, no matter your failure!

Failure is not an end, it's a detour!

Two of my favorite men in the Bible are Moses and Joseph; both were men who had detours that looked like failures.

In the case of Moses, the failure was his fault. As we see in Exodus 2, he was banished from the palace into the wilderness because he killed a man.

Joseph, on the other hand, didn't do anything wrong. Genesis 39 clearly says he never slept with Potiphar's wife and was imprisoned for a crime he never committed. But this was all part of God's plan. His detour was a God-designed plan to save the people of Israel and fulfill the purposes God had for his life.

If we could talk to both of these men, I'm sure they'd both say that there came a point where they felt like failures and honestly believed their lives were over. It was hopeless. They were lost and given up for dead with no chance of ever having a better life or achieving their God-given purpose.

To them and everyone around them, they'd failed. It. Was. Over.

Yet, in God's eyes it was just a detour.

It was part of their journey to becoming who He wanted them to be and fulfilling His purpose for their life.

As I was going on my own journey through climbing Mt. Failure, I drew encouragement from the lives of these men and others like them. I hung on to the truth that even though it looked like I'd failed and so many people were more than happy that my perfect family had a failure, in God's eyes it was just a detour.

Honestly, I knew in my heart that God had led me home and He had to have a plan. Even though I couldn't see it and there were times when I gave up hope and decided, "Okay, this is how the rest of my life is going to be," time proved the truth - that it was only a detour.

What I've learned is that whether we create our own failure or God leads us to it, if we allow Him to work in our lives, He can turn any failure into a detour that will bring glory and honor to Him.

Never Waste a Failure

The determining factor in whether your failure is the end or just a detour is ultimately up to you.

You see, one of the things I've learned over the years is that there are two ways to approach a failure or a "timeout."

You can sit back, be angry, pout, and essentially wait for God to move, or you can make the most of it.

Thanks to the counsel of my mom, I chose to make the most of it.

How do you do this?

1. Choose to spend time with Jesus and in the Word of God

When I came home from college, I was like a starving man. My heart was broken, and I was filled with confusion. Yet, I knew where I needed to go for answers. I needed God.

During my years of "failure," I spent hours with God and in His Word because I knew that I needed this more than anything else in my life. So I set aside specific amounts of time to spend in prayer and reading and studying God's Word. As I grew closer to God, His Word changed me.

The truth is that time spent with God or in the Bible is never wasted. It's always an investment. I always get so frustrated when I'm talking to someone who is in a situation similar to mine, and I ask, *"Are you praying? Are you reading the Bible?"* and they say, *"No."*

Why not?

This is a basic fundamental principle. I'll be honest and say that continuing to ignore these things may extend your own personal wilderness experience or it may give you a permanent wilderness residence.

I can also promise you this----if you will commit to pursuing prayer and God's Word---even if your circumstances don't change, YOU WILL.

So make the most of this time and spend time with Jesus and God's Word.

2. Allow God to Heal the Issues in Your Heart

Although I did not see it at the time, I can now look back and see that God ordained that time in my life for me to overcome the issues of my heart and be healed and delivered.

Still, it didn't magically happen.

I had to choose to spend hours alone with God, praying through the issues of my heart, remembering things I didn't want to remember.

Then came the choice to forgive my dad whether he was repentant or not.

I had to choose to study the Bible to learn new behavioral patterns that I could apply to my life.

As a family and individually, we spent a lot of time in counseling and working with a minister trained in spiritual deliverance. There were so many knots that needed to be untied from all the years of lies, deceit, and abuse.

We did a lot of talking, and individually, we all did a lot of journaling.

The healing and overcoming wasn't magical by any means. It took a lot of work and, honestly, constantly choosing over and over again that I would allow God to take me through this entire process of overcoming the past and setting me free.

Even though it was the hardest time in my life, I have absolutely no regrets that I chose to allow God to take this time in my life and set me free from my past. Without a speck of doubt, it was one of the best choices I made in my life.

Why?

Because I couldn't become the man God wanted me to be or do any of the things He wanted me to do until the lies and abuse that were scrambling my heart and mind were healed.

Until I dealt with my past, I was broken. I couldn't write a book or deliver a sermon. All I had to offer God or anyone else was my brokenness---a twisted, distorted version of the man God had originally created. When I chose to agree with God and allow Him to take me through the process of overcoming my past, God was able to heal my brokenness and replace it with wholeness and the opportunity to finally find my identity in Him. That's when things really started to change.

I have a friend who went through a time of failure. During this time, I thoroughly believe God wanted him to deal with some heart issues, sins, and attitudes he had that were tripping him up. But instead of doing this, the man did everything he could to prove he wasn't a failure. Eventually, he forced a door open to get him out of his situation, but he didn't change at all. I really worry for this man that he will stumble back into failure because he never dealt with the issues that got him there in the first place.

Why? Because I know the enemy will try and get us trapped back into a "failure mindset." He has tried this with me.

I don't want that for anyone reading this chapter. Please take this seriously. Allow God to heal the issues inside of you that caused the failure so you can move forward, free of it for good, as you gain victory over Mt. Failure.

3. Learn Everything You Can

It's important to realize that even while all this was going on in my spiritual life and the life of my family, we weren't just sitting around praying and singing hymns all day. I was also receiving an education in more practical areas.

You see, I came home to a mom who wasn't just passionate about God, but she was a very strong, capable woman who could do anything she put her mind to.

My mom saw each task and every challenge presented to her in life as an adventure—an opportunity to learn something new and try something new. Whether it was a spiritual challenge or a home repair project, her attitude was always, *"Okay God, we've finished that adventure—What's next?"*

While she was mentoring me, she was determined to pass this attitude on to me. I have to say that through the years, we had a lot of adventures as our home began needing a lot of repairs. After bringing in a few contractors for estimates, we began to realize that our entire family would be doing a lot of the work ourselves.

At first, we started off with easy projects, painting and wallpapering. Then we took the paneling down in my bedroom with the intention of painting the walls. To our surprise, when we got into the project we found that when the paneling was originally hung, they drew red lines from the floor to the ceiling every time there was a stud. So that's when we learned to drywall.

In time, the projects became more and more challenging. At one point, we converted our back porch into a laundry room for my mom. That's when I learned about framing, flooring, insulating, masonry, and siding.

One of the projects I'm proudest of is the time we needed to replace our toilet! I found a book on plumbing, and following their instructions, I removed the old toilet and installed the new one. I was so proud that I could do this plumbing job!

As God continued to allow our house to need repairs, I began to enjoy the challenges, and the sense of accomplishment that came from the finished product. I began to look at life as an adventure and enjoy the ride.

We didn't just learn about home repairs:

• We learned how to properly manage money.

• I taught myself how to do video production and website design.

• I began polishing my skills as a writer and speaker.

• I worked on my people skills which were sorely lacking!

• I learned to stop expecting to be served and started serving others around me.

• I learned that no job is below me and to do my best at whatever job I was doing.

- I learned to be hardworking and to pay attention to every little detail. As my mom said a million times, "If you're going to do a job, do it well."

- I learned how to have strong healthy relationships.

- I learned how to be a kind, gentle man with a servant's heart.

None of the ten years were wasted. Little did I know that I'd eventually use everything I was learning when God miraculously opened the door for me to enter into ministry.

You see, nothing is ever wasted in God's kingdom. The more you learn, the more you are able to invest into God's kingdom. So during your time of failure, don't just sit around waiting for it to be over---learn all you can. The more you learn, the more you are able to invest in God's kingdom.

During your time of failure don't just sit around waiting for it to be over---learn all you can. The more you learn the more you are able to invest in God's kingdom.

Take classes. Learn a skill. Increase your abilities. Understand that God's plan for your life may look drastically different than anything you ever imagined and be prepared for anything!

4. Don't Make Stupid Mistakes

Have you ever thought about what would have happened if Joseph had slept with Potiphar's wife?

Honestly, it was an option.

He could have become angry with God and thought, *"This stinks. I was the good son and yet You let this happen to me? I'm just going to do whatever I want---I deserve it and living right doesn't pay off anyway."*

But let's be honest....Joseph would not have been the eventual leader of Egypt if he'd made this choice.

It's the same for us. Just because God allows a detour in our lives doesn't give us an excuse to fool around with sin. Instead, we need to walk CLOSER to God and lead a holier life.

I'll be honest and say that I've seen it happen too many times.

People say they are in one of God's "holding patterns," and yet they are living a life of sin.

Guess what?

Sin is not going to lead you to God's perfect will for your life; it's going to lead you away from it. You might be on a detour, but it's in the wrong direction. Choosing to sin will never lead you to the life God has for you.

During my own journey through failure, I was very committed to not just living as close to Jesus as possible but also to overcoming and resisting sin's temptations.

Were there days when I wanted to chuck it all and just go have some fun?

Absolutely. But I didn't because I was committed to following God's plan for my life whether I stayed in my wilderness forever or whether He eventually opened the doors for ministry.

If you're going through a similar experience, I encourage you, do not do stupid things.

Don't choose the pleasures of sin for a season. It's not worth it. Instead, choose to obey God's Word and live a pure, holy life before Him. Allow Him the opportunity to work in your life. Don't close the door on your own possibilities.

Can I add one final thought?

5. Learn to Enjoy Your Life

I remember my mom telling me during this time in my life that I needed to relax and enjoy it. She said years later I'd look back on this time and remember the quiet, the peace, and the time alone with Jesus and actually miss it.

Honestly, I thought she was crazy.

But she was right.

The truth is that this time in life is precious. It's a once in a lifetime experience where life is kind of "on hold" while the God of the Universe works on your heart. And now I find myself telling the same thing to people in similar situations…some day you will look back on this time as the best in your life. Then I chuckle as they give me that, "You're nuts" look I used to give my mom when she'd say the same to me.

It's also important that you enjoy the people who are in your life at this time. Don't spend your days and nights wishing you were somewhere else, but make the most of today. Trust me; it will be gone way too fast.

Looking back on my own life, I can see that the life I was dreading on graduation morning, was actually a blessing.

Although the detour took me through humiliation, embarrassment, failure, and pain, it also filled my life with healing, deliverance, the love of my family, a restored relationship with my mom, peace, and joy beyond anything I could ever imagine.

It was the exact road I needed to be on to take me where I needed to be.

The same is true for you if God leads you down this road.

Don't resent it, instead embrace it. Take full advantage of it and see what amazing things God has in store on the other side of your failure.

Don't let the enemy trap you in failure again. Whenever the voice of failure tries to rear it's ugly head again, stand up to Mt. Failure and say, *"No, I am not sliding back down this mountain again. I am serving God faithfully and doing what He called me to do. I refuse to accept these lies!"* Then I dust yourself off and get back to work!

Your failure is not the end of the trail for you. Don't just settle in at the base of Mt. Failure and sulk. It's time to climb! Gain victory, and don't slide back down again.

Dear Heavenly Father,

Please forgive me for allowing my past failures to dictate my future victories. Help me see that nothing is wasted in Your kingdom, not even failure.

Father, take my biggest failure and use it for Your glory. Help me use this experience to deal with the sin and pain in my heart. Help me learn everything I can during this time. Help me appreciate this time of rebooting from failure. Help me to enjoy it and embrace, and give me strength to rebound and move forward once again. In Jesus' name, Amen!

GROUP STUDY QUESTIONS:

1. What have you failed at in life?

2. How has this failure shaped your life?

3. Why is it important to allow God to heal your heart after failure?

4. How can we enjoy our life during times of failure?

5. After reading this chapter, what is one thing you will put into practice or one thing you will change in your life?

6. How can we, as a group, help you do this?

-CHAPTER EIGHT-

MT. BETRAYAL

I have always enjoyed studying the great men of history and reading their stories. One of the men I enjoy studying is George Washington. I especially enjoy reading about his time as the leader of the Continental Army.

Leading this group of undisciplined soldiers was at times very frustrating for General Washington. He learned to surround himself with only the best men who were devoted to the cause. He put his 100% trust in them, and he expected the same.

General Washington had one general in particular who he respected and trusted. This general bravely fought to defeat the British at Ridgefield and Danbury. He helped capture Fort Ticonderoga. He led the invasion of Canada. He single-handedly rallied the troops at the Battle of Saratoga while enduring a crippling leg injury. Without this general's leadership and military contributions, few believe we would have won our independence.

Who was this beloved general and friend to General Washington?

General Benedict Arnold.

That's right! The man who General Washington respected and trusted turned out to be the poster child for betrayal. No other person besides Judas Iscariot is so synonymous with betrayal as Benedict Arnold.

Can you imagine the blow it was to General Washington when he learned of Benedict Arnold's treason?

The sensation of being stabbed in the back must have been horrific! There is no worse feeling than having a friend, a close, personal friend who you trust stab you in the back. How do you respond to such betrayal?

In this chapter, we are going to look at the mountain that no one likes to think about but most people will face at some point in their lives…how to respond to betrayal.

Like General Washington, many have encountered people who they trusted to have their backs, only to have them jam a knife deep into the very back they were supposedly protecting. Nothing is more painful than the betrayal of a friend. David sums up the pain in Psalms 55 when he says,

We cannot react in a vengeful or hateful way. We cannot try and destroy our attacker or pay them back for the evil they did to us. This is the action of a carnal man, and we are men following God.

My insides are turned inside out; specters of death have me down. I shake with fear, I shudder from head to foot……This isn't the neighborhood bully mocking me—I could take that. This isn't a foreign devil spitting invective—I could tune that out. It's you! We grew up together! You! My best friend! Those long hours of leisure as we walked arm in arm, God a third party to our conversation. (The Message)

Attacks from a stranger or acquaintance are hard to deal with, but when the attacks and betrayal come at the hands of a friend or loved one, it is unbearable pain. So how do we get back up? How do we respond when someone we loved and trusted like a brother stabs us in the back and twists the knife? How do we move on from Mt. Betrayal?

Let's start by saying how not to respond. This piece of advice is one of the hardest things in the world not to do, yet a man of God has to do it.

We cannot react in a vengeful or hateful way. We cannot try and destroy our attacker or pay them back for the evil they have done to us. This is the action of a carnal man, and we are men following God. So, as hard as it is, we have to respond in a Christlike manner.

Believe me, I know it is REALLY hard not to do this! It is what our sinful nature screams out to do.

- We want to tell all of our friends and fellow church-goers how evil our spouse who cheated on us is.

- We want our friends who stabbed us in the back when we needed them most to suffer and experience this same pain.

- We want vindication when someone spreads hateful lies about us.

- We want to destroy the person who broke our confidence and shared with the world what we thought was a private moment between friends.

- We revenge, and we want them to pay!

I have experienced betrayal in my life. I have had close friends take personal letters and emails, edit them, and use them against me to lie about me. I've had people I have invested in and poured my life into completely abandon me when God called me to a new area of ministry. My own father betrayed our family when he lived a secret double life.

I know firsthand the pain of betrayal. It hurts, and it makes us want to get even. But that's not how God wants us to act. He has a better way.

Luckily for us, the Bible gives us an example of how Jesus responded to being stabbed in the back by a close friend. As we examine Jesus' example, we will see four ways to respond when facing devastating betrayal from a friend.

Most people, even nonbelievers, instantly know who it was who betrayed Jesus. I mean, just the other day I was watching a television show in which one person wanted to let the other person know their actions were a betrayal.

What vicious name did they call the person? "Judas."

Yes, the name Judas has become synonymous with betrayal, treachery, and backstabbing. We all know that Judas was the man that betrayed Jesus and handed Him over to be crucified. Still, a study of these events will show us, not only the act of betrayal, but the way we are to handle our betrayers.

You see, even though everything we are going to study in this chapter takes place BEFORE Judas betrayed Jesus, we have to realize that Jesus knew Judas would betray Him. Jesus knew Judas, the man He had called to follow Him, the man He invested three years of discipleship and mentorship into, the man He had loved like a brother, the very one He trusted to handle the "ministry purse strings," was going to betray Him.

I remember once watching a TV show where people were going to do a live reenactment of Da Vinci's "The Last Supper" painting. The person who was going to be Jesus was really into the part, hanging out with his "disciples" and doing fun activities. That is until he met the person who played Judas Iscariot.

The man playing Jesus immediately shunned "Judas." He didn't ask him to go to dinner or bowling with the rest of the group, and eventually ended up rolling around the floor in a brawl with the man. While hilarious to watch, it is also the exact opposite of what the real Son of God did when dealing with a close friend who would betray

Him. So, knowing full well Judas was going to stab Him in the back, how did Jesus treat Judas?

1. Jesus Did Good to Him

> *It was just before the Passover Festival. Jesus knew that the hour had come for Him to leave this world and go to the Father. Having loved His own who were in the world, He loved them to the end.*
>
> *The evening meal was in progress, and the devil had already prompted Judas, the son of Simon Iscariot, to betray Jesus. Jesus knew that the Father had put all things under his power, and that he had come from God and was returning to God; so he got up from the meal, took off his outer clothing, and wrapped a towel around his waist. After that, he poured water into a basin and began to wash his disciples' feet, drying them with the towel that was wrapped around him. John 13:1-5 (NIV)*

This passage is quite clear that Jesus knew Judas was about to commit the ultimate betrayal against Him, yet He still dropped to His knees and washed the slime and filth off the feet of this slimy man. Jesus didn't lord over Judas or put him in his place. He didn't treat him cruelly or push him away. He, instead, put on a servant's heart and did good to him.

When dealing with a betrayer, the hardest thing in the world to do is not to repay evil with evil. Yet, this is what God calls us to do.

If Jesus, the Son of God, could bring Himself to wash the filthy feet of His betrayer, we can do good to our betrayers as well. When dealing with a betrayer, the hardest thing in the world to do is to not repay evil with evil. Yet, this is what God calls us to do. Instead, we need to do good to those who treat us badly.

2. Jesus Loved Him

After he had said this, Jesus was troubled in spirit and testified, "Very truly I tell you, one of you is going to betray me."

His disciples stared at one another, at a loss to know which of them he meant. One of them, the disciple whom Jesus loved, was reclining next to him. Simon Peter motioned to this disciple and said, "Ask him which one he means."

Leaning back against Jesus, he asked him, "Lord, who is it?"

Jesus answered, "It is the one to whom I will give this piece of bread when I have dipped it in the dish." Then, dipping the piece of bread, he gave it to Judas, the son of Simon Iscariot. As soon as Judas took the bread, Satan entered into him. John 13:21-27 (NIV)

Alfred Edersheim states that Judas had the seat of honor next to Jesus, on His left.[1] Other commentaries say that this passage shows that Judas was sitting next to Jesus at the table; if he was in arm's reach of Jesus to receive the bread, then it meant that he was sitting next to Him. Plus, Judas was privy to the discussion about who the betrayer was, whereas most of the disciples at the table were not. After all, most of the disciples at the table did not think that Jesus, when he told Judas to do his task quickly, was referring to Judas' betrayal of Jesus, but rather to Judas' responsibilities as the group's treasurer (John 13:26-29; cp. Matthew 26:25). Only John and Judas were privy to the discussion about Judas being the betrayer, indicating that they probably sat next to Jesus.

Interesting, but what does it have to do with dealing with a betrayer? Well, if Judas was sitting next to Jesus, it means that Jesus gave Judas, His betrayer, the seat of honor above all of the other disciples. Sitting next to the Master was a high privilege.

Jesus showed love to Judas by treating Him this way, knowing full well what the rest of the night entailed. He did everything He could to help Judas see he was loved. We need to do the same.

106

Now let's get real: there is no way in the world we are going to like the person who betrays us. It would be unnatural and even unhealthy, if we did. Still, we need to love them and see that our struggle is not against flesh and blood.

Reality is that Satan was controlling Judas. Granted, Judas gave ground to be used, but the attack was spiritual. The same is true in our situation. Our betrayers are being used by the enemy to attack us and stop us in our tracks. We have to show Christlike love for our enemies and not treat them with hate. We don't have to "like" them, but we do have to love them.

3. Jesus Forgave Him

While he was still speaking, Judas, one of the Twelve, arrived. With him was a large crowd armed with swords and clubs, sent from the chief priests and the elders of the people. Now the betrayer had arranged a signal with them: "The one I kiss is the man; arrest him." Going at once to Jesus, Judas said, "Greetings, Rabbi!" and kissed him. Jesus replied, "Do what you came for, friend."
- Matthew 26:47-50 (NIV)

How could Jesus call Judas "friend?" I believe it was because Jesus had already forgiven Judas for what He did. He didn't call him a name that implied anger, hate or unforgiveness. Instead, He called him "friend."

Like Jesus, we need to also forgive the one who betrays us. Why? Because all unforgiveness does is holds us in bondage and captive to our betrayers. However, when we

Unforgiveness holds us in bondage and captive to the one who betrayed us. However, when we forgive them, we free OURSELVES from their actions. So we need to forgive them.

forgive them, we free OURSELVES from their actions. So we need to forgive them.

4. Jesus Let Him Go

As soon as Judas took the bread, Satan entered into him. So Jesus told him, "What you are about to do, do quickly." - John 13:27 (NIV)

Ok, this event happened previously to the last event we discussed, but I wanted to end with this point. Jesus did everything He could to help Judas and work through the betrayal, but when push came to shove, He had to release Judas. He had to part ways with His betrayer.

While we need to be sure to show love, forgiveness, and have a heart of reconciliation with our betrayer, if they refuse to accept our love and forgiveness, then you have to move on and let them go. The relationship cannot continue. God commands us to love and forgive, but He doesn't command us to be a whipping post. We do not have to continue a relationship with a betrayer who refuses to work things out and deal with the issues. We have to let them go and end the relationship.

I guess I list this point to relieve some guilt many people feel who don't want to continue a relationship with a betrayer. As long as you treat them with love, dignity, and respect, you do not have to continue in a relationship with them. Don't let them or anyone else place guilt on you for this. It is not your fault as long as you handled yourself in a godly way.

That is what this entire chapter is all about.

Betrayal comes in all forms and sizes. Most of us have experienced it or will experience it at some point in our lives. We have no control over how our betrayer acts, but we do have control over our actions.

We need to respond in a Christlike way. We need to follow Jesus' example and show love, forgiveness, and goodness to our enemies. However, we don't need to be a doormat. It is okay to pull back from the relationship. What is important is to respond like Jesus responded. When we can do this, we can gain victory over our Mt. Betrayal.

"But Jamie, the pain of the betrayal is still so strong. I am really angry at this person."

I get it. As Christians, we have to be honest with ourselves when it comes to deep wounds, and there is no deeper wound than when a friend or loved one stabs you in the back.

Honestly, the wound won't go away immediately. You can't expect it of yourself, demanding that your heart be instantly healed so you can be "super-Christian." That is like telling yourself, with two broken legs, *"Now go run a marathon---it's what God wants."*

Emotional pain is just as real as physical pain, and it takes just as much time, if not longer, to heal. In traumatic situations, all we can ask of ourselves as humans is to move in the right direction. Practically, what does that mean?

We must make the choice to forgive on a daily basis. Sometimes this simply means saying, *"Heavenly Father, I choose to forgive them today, now please help my actions to follow my choice."*

• Choose not to retaliate.

• Treat the offender with dignity and respect.

• Allow yourself time to work through your feelings.

• Talk through your pain with God, and if necessary, a trusted friend or counselor.

• Keep moving forward in the right direction---but don't demand instant results.

Every small step forward is progress; just never stop moving forward.

Also, be sure to avoid "burying" a deep wound under the guise of forgiveness. Some people avoid facing the pain of their emotions by saying, *"I forgave them."* However, if they didn't really take the time to face their emotions and come to a place of resolve, they only buried the hurt.

This is dangerous because buried hurts only stay buried so long, and then one day, they explode---often hitting innocent victims nearby with shrapnel. It's much better to allow yourself time to work through deep hurts, pray through deep hurts, and have them heal properly then quickly cover them with a Band-Aid pretending they aren't serious. It's the healthiest, holiest way.

If you consistently face your emotional pain, take it to God, ask Him to help you to forgive---even if it's only a little bit at a time, your heart will heal. Slowly, but surely. But that's normal for healing---a broken bone doesn't heal overnight. It takes a specified amount of time before you can use it again---even then it won't be back to normal for at least a year after the break. We need to allow broken hearts the same understanding—work toward healing while understanding that full healing takes time.

Dear Heavenly Father,

You know my situation. You know the pain and devastation that I am feeling over the loss of this relationship due to betrayal. You know my worldly desire is to seek revenge, hurt, and destroy this one who has betrayed me. Help me to not give into these desires. Instead, help me respond like Jesus.

Help me to show Christlike love and forgiveness towards them. Help me to be able to let the relationship go and move forward with You. Help me defeat Mt. Betrayal!

In Jesus' name, Amen.

GROUP STUDY QUESTIONS:

1. Why can't we get back at or take revenge against someone who betrays us?

2. What good thing can you do for your betrayer?

3. Why is it sometimes necessary to let the relationship go?

4. Which part of our discussion on forgiveness stood out the most to you?

5. After reading this chapter, what is one thing you will put into practice or one thing you will change in your life?

6. How can we, as a group, help you do this?

-CHAPTER NINE-

MT. BROKEN RELATIONSHIPS

There is one sure truth in life…we need other people. No one can go through life alone or without interacting with others. We need each other. However, sometimes our relationships with others don't always go the way we want them to go, and sometimes our relationships end up broken.

Like it or not:

• Marriages sometimes end.

• Business partners can encounter problems and go their separate directions.

• At times, friendships explode in unhealthy ways.

• Kids leave home and don't always look back.

• People storm off from their churches when they become angry.

On and on the list goes. Because people are human beings born with sinful natures, at some point we inevitably have relationships that end up broken and shattered. As someone who has experienced broken relationships in my life, I know the hurt and pain this causes. It is excruciatingly painful.

However, we can't let this pain cause us to lie down and seek shelter in the shadow of Mt. Broken Relationships. God called us to enter into His Promised Land! You can conquer this mountain.

As I said, I personally have dealt with broken relationships in my life. In our chapter on Mt. Shame, we discussed that my shame was how I treated my mom growing up. Our relationship was a very broken relationship. But I know firsthand that God has the power to heal a broken relationship! He healed and restored my broken relationship with my mom, and He can do the same for you.

In this chapter, we are going to look at both sides of a broken relationship...what to do if it is your fault, and what to do if you're the victim of the broken relationship.

In my relationship with my mom, I was the breaker of the relationship. I was the one who went to college and pushed my family as far away as I could. When God brought me back home after college, my relationship with my family was still really rocky, and to be honest, I didn't do very much to fix it. Then I had the "punching-the-door" experience that started my spiritual breakthrough so that God could remake me into the man He wanted me to be.

Part of this process was working to restore my broken relationship with my mom. I had done a lot of damage to our relationship over the years, so I had to work hard to restore the relationship. It didn't break overnight, so a quick fix wasn't going to happen either. But the steps I took helped us bridge the gap that developed between us, and I believe these steps will do the same for you.

So what are they?

1. Admit Your Part of the Problem.

The first thing I had to do was own responsibility for the problem.

Yes, my dad was a huge cause of the divide between my mom and me, but I couldn't keep excusing my behavior and pawning the responsibility off onto him. I was unable to break free of my sinful behavior and destructive habits until I was able to get my eyes off of my dad and onto myself. I had to stop saying, *"My dad was abusive,"* and start saying, *"I am an abusive man, and I need help!"* I had to stop blaming him for my issues. I had to let him off the hook and accept responsibility for my own sin.

Just because my dad was abusive to me didn't give me the right to be abusive to my mom. I had to admit this sin to myself and acknowledge I had a problem. I had to deal with myself before I tried to deal with my mom, or else I would have addressed the broken

Healing started with me admitting I had a problem.

relationship in the same manner that I had done when I had broken it. Healing started with me admitting I had a problem.

2. Seek God's Forgiveness and Reconciliation.

Step two is asking God to forgive you for destroying the relationship. Ask Him to transform your life and make you into a new man.

For me, I had to ask for forgiveness from the abusive behavior I had committed towards my mom. Some of you may need to ask to be forgiven for lying, cheating, walking away, stealing, etc. The point is that after you own your part of the broken relationship, ask God to forgive you and start working on changing.

3. Ask the Other Person to Forgive You.

While this step seems simple, it is in no way easy. It will require a humble, broken spirit and a willingness to be vulnerable, but a loving man of God will do it in order to restore the relationship.

Sit down with the other person if possible and talk openly, honestly and humbly with them. Do not be judgmental or defensive.

Tell them you want to ask for their forgiveness for the mistakes you made in the relationship. Be specific. Don't be vague. Remember, you are fighting for the relationship…don't let pride interfere.

What do you ask forgiveness for? Here are some examples:

If the broken relationship is with a child because of a divorce, ask them for forgiveness for your not being able to protect them from all of the hurt and pain that comes along with a divorce.

If you were an abusive man, ask them to forgive you for your cruel and abusive behavior. Explain your anger was out of control, but Jesus has set you free. You now want to ask them to forgive you for the damage you did to their soul. Let them know that you realize you were wrong, and you are heartbroken and regretful for the damage your behavior caused.

If the shattered relationship was because you were unfaithful to your wife, ask her to forgive you. Let her know you deeply regret the immoral sin you committed. Get across to her that you were struggling with sexual sins, but now God has set you free. You now want to restore your relationship with her.

These are just a few of the many examples of ways to repent. The point is that you need to humble yourself and become vulnerable. The other person/persons needs to see you are broken and sorrowful. You may want to share with them the issues from your own past that led to the sin in your life. Share with them if you were abused as a child, and how the anger from that abuse spilled over into you being abusive. Maybe your dad was trapped in sexual sin, and the pattern continued into your life.

However, when you do this, MAKE SURE YOU LET THEM KNOW YOU ARE NOT SAYING THIS AS AN EXCUSE OR TO PASS BLAME ON SOMEONE ELSE! You need to let them know that you have come to the place where you do not blame your parents or anyone else for your sinful behavior. You take full responsibility for your actions, you have repented to God, and now you want to restore your broken relationship with them.

Let them know that you're sharing this with them to let them see this isn't just a flip repentance. Instead, you want them to see that you have reflected on your issues, realized the cause of them, are truly repentant of your actions, and are working to change and overcome.

4. Don't Demand Trust, Rebuild It.

It is important for you to admit your sins and ask for forgiveness. However, you can't force them to forgive you. You have to realize they may not forgive you right away, or ever. You may need to prove yourself to them first.

When I first started the process of rebuilding the relationship with my mom, she didn't immediately jump back into the relationship. Because she was a godly woman who believed in forgiveness, she said she forgave me. Her trust on the other hand, was a completely different story.

I had to work to regain her trust. This is why Step 2 is so important. You have to allow God to make you into a new man. Then you have to allow the other person time to realize you actually have changed.

I had to prove myself to my mom. She had to see that my newfound devotion to God and allowing Him to work on me was real, not just a get-out-of-jail-free card. She had to see me respond differently to situations and events in life. Trust didn't come until she saw I was serious about changing and was becoming a new person.

It will take a lot of hard work on your part, but God can restore the relationship.

Did I like the fact that her trust wasn't instant? Heck no!

But I understood that it took years to destroy the relationship, so I couldn't expect it to rebuild instantly.

Counselors say it takes an average of seven years for trust to be restored in a marriage after an affair. While this stat relates to a specific kind of broken relationship, it demonstrates the need to be patient and realize it will take time to restore the broken trust.

It will take a lot of hard work on your part, but God can restore the relationship. Be faithful, do your part, and allow the other person to see the difference.

5. Give the Other Person Time to Heal.

While it is important to give the person time to trust you again, it is equally important for you to give the person time to heal.

You can't expect them to instantly get over it. A broken arm or a shattered leg doesn't heal overnight; it takes time to heal. A heart is the same way.

Allow the person time and space to work through their feelings. If you don't, true healing of the relationship will never take place.

What if you are not the person who broke the relationship? How do you go about conquering Mt. Broken Relationships?

Well, I have experience with this side of the equation as well. As you probably figured out reading this book, my dad and I don't have the ideal relationship.

Why? Because he wants it that way. That's as blunt as I can put it. He hasn't done any of the above steps, and while I have done what I can to fix our relationship, I can't force him to want a healed relationship.

Maybe you find yourself in a similar situation. What can you do? Well, here is what I have done.

1. Forgive.

When it came to forgiving my Dad, I struggled with questions like:

- What do I do with all the emotional pain that I still feel?

- Why can't I just forget and pretend that things are all 'hunky dory?'

- How can I fix a relationship with someone who is content with the current relationship?

- How do I forgive someone who isn't sorry and doesn't want to change?

Then, of course, I'd feel guilty because I knew that God wanted me to forgive. Over and over again this roller coaster ride continued. Until I began to understand what forgiveness was and what it was not.

This changed my life!

First of all, forgiveness is not condoning the other person's behavior as acceptable or no big deal.

You see, one of the reasons that forgiveness was so hard for me is that I saw forgiveness as a get-out-of-jail-free card for people who weren't really sorry and didn't want to change their lives. The truth is that you don't want to tell the person who hurt you and changed your life that everything they did is alright.

One thing that helped me was when the Holy Spirit showed me that to forgive you have to acknowledge that the other person hurt you and damaged you. You admit that they were wrong. An offense occurred---what they did wasn't alright---that's why you need to forgive them.

When I realized that forgiveness wasn't saying, "It's okay that you did this or it's no big deal," that's when I could put things into perspective. You stop blaming yourself for the pain inside of your heart.

Here are some other things to keep in mind about forgiveness:

1. Forgiveness doesn't mean you have to forget.

Realistically, you can't forget what happened. It's part of your story. I mean, how could I "forget" decades of my life? You can't.

What forgiveness will do is heal your heart and take away the pain when you remember. That's how I can write this book or tell my story in a sermon—because it doesn't hurt anymore. I can't forget the facts, but I no longer have to live trapped in the pain.

2. Forgiveness doesn't mean you don't bring it up again.

Talking about issues is the key to freedom. Talking is healthy. Suppressing hurts, and keeping secrets is unhealthy. God wants us to be healthy.

3. Forgiveness doesn't mean you have to put your heart on the line to be hurt again by someone who is unrepentant and unchanged.

Just because God commands us to forgive does not mean that He wants us to allow people to abuse us, demean us, or diminish our dignity without establishing boundaries.

That would be unwise. God wants His children to be wise. Healthy boundaries are choices that you make to proceed in a safer, healthier, more beneficial manner with the goal of living a peaceful life.

Honestly, once the Holy Spirit removed my fear of forgiveness by showing me what forgiveness was not, then I was able to understand what forgiveness is and start experiencing its healing power in my life.

Over the years, what I've come to learn is that forgiveness is not about the other person. Forgiveness is a gift you give yourself.

So what is forgiveness?

Forgiveness is a choice that we make to follow God and to choose to forgive someone who hurt us.

Forgiveness is the ointment that keeps you from being tied up in knots of hate, anger, and resentment.

The truth is that as long as you don't forgive them, they are still hurting you and controlling your life. You are still the other person's prisoner. When you can say, *"I know you were wrong, but I forgive you,"* you are releasing yourself from all the power the other person has over you. That opens the door for God's healing power to do a miracle in your heart.

Forgiveness is about setting yourself free to experience God's love and healing regardless of what happens with the other person.

Think of it like this: The person who hurt you took a can of paint and threw it at you for no good reason. They made a cruel decision or decisions, and they were wrong.

Forgiveness is about setting yourself free to experience God's love and healing regardless of what happens to the other person.

However, you are the one covered in paint. Unless you wash the paint off of your skin and your clothes, that paint isn't going to go away.

Forgiveness is the first step in washing the pain from your skin.

Forgiveness is saying, *"I'm not going to let your choices affect the rest of my life. I am going to do whatever is necessary to pursue healing and freedom."*

The truth is that forgiveness is a crucial step in healing. It is impossible to heal without it. Even though it isn't always easy, your personal journey to healing and freedom cannot start until you make the decision that you are going to forgive.

2. Pray For Them.

Begin to pray for the person. Now, I am not saying pray that God gets even with them! Trust me, I know this is how our sinful human hearts will lead us to pray! But a heart that forgives will pray for God to bless them.

In our chapter on betrayal, I mentioned my experienced with a friend who took emails, edited them, and used them against me. This broken relationship was very painful, and trust me, I prayed lots of *"God get 'em"* prayers. But this didn't change my heart.

My heart didn't change until I started praying for God to bless them.

Praying for someone who needs to be forgiven is like putting healing ointment on your own wound. As you pray, God is using your prayer to not only change that person, but He's using it to heal your heart.

Jesus commanded us to bless those who despitefully use us. We need to follow this pattern. Ask God to bless the person, provide for their needs, and help them become all that He wants them to be.

I believe that one of the reasons God commands us to do this is because, in time, it is hard to feel hatred and unforgiveness while praying for the person's good.

3. Do Something Nice for the Person.

We talked about this before in the chapter on anger, but it's worth repeating.

Luke 6:27-34 says:

> *But to you who are listening I say: Love your enemies, do good to those who hate you, Bless those who curse you, pray for those who mistreat you.*
>
> *If someone slaps you on one cheek, turn to them the other also.*
>
> *If someone takes your coat, do not withhold your shirt from them.*
>
> *Give to everyone who asks you, and if anyone takes what belongs to you, do not demand it back.*
>
> *Do to others as you would have them do to you.*

If you love those who love you, what credit is that to you? Even sinners love those who love them.

And if you do good to those who are good to you, what credit is that to you?

Even sinners do that. And if you lend to those from whom you expect repayment, what credit is that to you? Even sinners lend to sinners, expecting to be repaid in full.

But love your enemies, do good to them, and lend to them without expecting to get anything back.

Then your reward will be great, and you will be children of the Most High, because he is kind to the ungrateful and wicked. Be merciful, just as your Father is merciful. (NIV)

I'm going to be very honest and say that this was not easy for me to do with my dad---especially after my mom went to Heaven.

The truth is that after she died, we were done. Our goal was to get away from my dad and never look back. Maybe a Christmas card---maybe not.

I was done. I'd had enough of the pain, the abuse, and his unwillingness to change. There were days when even just looking at him or having to talk to him as we were grieving and remembering the horrific way he treated Mom were almost impossible.

My plan was to get out the door as soon as I could. Only God had another plan.

It wasn't long until the Holy Spirit spoke to my heart and said, *"No, you're not leaving. You are going to stay and show My love to your dad."*

Are you kidding me?

How could God expect this?

Yet, it was as I obeyed and continued showing love to my dad that

I healed.

Honestly, I believe this choice is the reason that my dad chose to go back to church and give Christianity another try. I truly believe if I would have left, he'd have chosen another direction.

Even more, it was out of this choice to forgive that my testimony was formed. I mean, how can we honestly say that God is able to heal and set people free through forgiveness if we are not willing to forgive?

Yet, today I can honestly say that if you forgive even when it's hard...even when the offense seems unforgivable...God can heal your heart.

Today, I am no longer walking around hurting, bitter and broken, but I am strong, healthy, and able to function — not out of a place of emotion, but from a rational perspective where I make intelligent choices and do the right thing.

The same can be true for you. As you allow the Holy Spirit to work in your life, not only will He heal your heart, but He'll work miraculously through your choice to touch the lives of other people.

Maybe God won't require you to go as far as He did me, but the verses we looked at above do show us we need to do good for the person, even if it is as simple as sending them a note or buying them a cup of coffee.

4. Accept that Forgiving Them Doesn't Always Mean the Relationship Will Be Restored.

Just because you forgive the person doesn't mean the relationship will be restored. That is a two person decision. Your responsibility is to forgive and let the results to God.

Forgiveness doesn't mean you allow the person to keep sinning against you.

Today as I write this chapter I can say in good conscience that through the power of the Holy Spirit, I have forgiven my dad.

However, my forgiveness is not a license for him to be abusive.

Although most of the dramatic outbursts and violent situations have stopped since he went back to church, there are still times when his manipulative, controlling tactics of emotional abuse try to resurface. When this happens, I lovingly confront him and let him know it is unacceptable and WILL NOT continue. However, I don't allow hatred, anger, or unforgiveness to take root inside of me, either.

For instance, recently my dad had an outburst. He meant to scare and intimidate us in order to get his own way.

But because of the healing power of Jesus in our lives, it didn't work out.

Instead of becoming afraid, losing our tempers or allowing anger, rage, or unforgiveness to consume us, I told him this behavior was unacceptable, and he had to stop and get control of himself. Then I went on with the rest of the day.

True forgiveness allows you to take a stand against the evil behavior while not allowing anger, bitterness and hate to consume you. That's the goal: your freedom and healing! Restoration is out of your hands…your spiritual health isn't.

Today, I don't know the story that led to your broken relationship. It may be more or less dramatic than mine, and you may feel like you have more or less to forgive. In the end, what matters for each of us is that forgiveness is a necessary ingredient to gaining freedom, joy, and healing in your life. There's no detour around it. Forgiveness is the only road to conquer Mt. Broken Relationships.

Broken relationships are difficult, painful mountains. Too many of God's people are stuck in the pain of broken relationships, marriages, friendships, and church relationships. No matter if we are the breakers or the ones broken, we can't stay stuck in the mire of these broken relationships. We have to climb!

We can conquer Mt. Broken Relationship in our lives.

Dear Heavenly Father,

You know the pain of broken relationships that I am living with in my life.

Pray this if you caused the broken relationship:

Please forgive me for the things that I have done to destroy this relationship. I confess the sin to You today and ask, not just for forgiveness, but for a restoration in my life. Help me to face myself, make changes, and start anew. Help me to be humble enough to ask the one I offended to forgive me. Help me not to expect or demand their trust and forgiveness, but to give them the time necessary to trust me again.

Pray this if you are the one the offense was against:

Father, please help me to forgive this person who hurt me and destroyed our relationship. Heal my heart and help me to forgive. Show me ways to show kindness to them, and help me realize that I can't change them, I can only work on my own heart.

Father, I no longer want to live at the foot of Mt. Broken Relationships. Help me to conquer this mountain and take my Promised Ground.

In Jesus' name, Amen.

GROUP STUDY QUESTIONS:

1. Do you have a broken relationship in your life?

2. Were you responsible for breaking the relationship?

3. Why is it important to seek forgiveness?

4. Why is it important to rebuild trust and to give the other person time to heal?

5. Which part of our discussion on forgiveness stood out the most to you?

6. After reading this chapter, what is one thing you will put into practice or one thing you will change in your life?

7. How can we, as a group, help you do this?

–Chapter Ten–

Mt. Debt

As we begin this chapter, I will be honest with you…when I was originally praying about what mountains God wanted to discuss in this book, I immediately felt we should talk about Mt. Debt. At first, I didn't think it was really a "spiritual" mountain that was keeping men from becoming everything God created them to be. But I put it on the list. Why?

Because God showed me why this topic was so important and how it fits so well into this book's theme. After all, we are encouraging men to be invincible, to climb their mountains and become what God created them to be, go where God called them to go, and do what God called them to do. What is one thing paramount on any man's mind when He considers a new career, a new location, taking a missions trip, investing time into other men, etc?

It is, *"Can I afford it?"*

Money and finances are a huge mountain that can keep us stuck and unable to move forward. Debt causes many men to stay sidelined spiritually. What do I mean?

Well, if you have a lot of debt, it can keep you from being able to do what God calls you to do. Say God says to you, *"I want you to take a different job that pays a little less but allows you to spend more time with your family."* If you are drowning in debt, you won't be able to do what God called you to do.

What if God lays it on your heart to be a financial supporter of a particular ministry or a project at church? If you are drowning in debt, you won't be able to walk on these waters.

Say God REALLY calls you to deep waters and calls you to leave your job and begin a life of ministry full time...it happens, I have seen it! Having debt will keep you from being able to do it.

There is a reason that Proverbs 22:7 says, *"The rich rule over the poor, and the borrower is slave to the lender."* I don't know about you, but I want to be God's servant, not servant to the person I owe money. I want to be able to do what God wants me to do, go where He wants me to go, and reach those He wants me to reach, and I don't ever want to let money or debt keep me from doing this.

(I want to make it clear before we go further, this chapter is discussing consumer debt, consciously choosing to spend money we don't have to get what we want...now! I understand not all debt is consumer debt. Some debt comes from sickness and medical bills, natural disasters, and other unforeseen circumstances that life throws at us. We are not discussing this form of debt, we are discussing consumer debt and choosing to live beyond our means.)

You may say, *"Well, if God calls me to do one of the things you mentioned, won't He supply the money and get me out of debt instantaneously?"*

My answer is a very blunt...NO!

Why do I say this?

Because God didn't create the debt, you did.

He didn't live beyond his means. We did. Actions have consequences, and it takes work and effort on our part to get out of debt. Why?

Because if God magically paid off our debt without change or effort on our part, we would soon find ourselves back into debt again. Money and numbers aren't the problem...our actions, attitudes, and spending habits are the problem. Until we change this, we won't change our finances.

Before we go into details on how to do this, I want to spend a short amount of time sharing my testimony with you and why I feel I am able to discuss climbing Mt. Debt. Again, I want to say I don't

Money and numbers aren't the problems...our actions, attitudes, and spending habits are the problem.

share this out of pain or anger at my dad. He knows I am sharing our testimony, and he has given permission for us to share it if it helps other men avoid his mistakes.

As I said before, I was raised in the church. In March of 1979, my mom made a personal commitment to Jesus when I was a ripe old age of 2. When she got saved, she was all in. Her life changed that day, from then on she tried to live every part of her life in a way that would please Jesus. This included her financial life. She dedicated herself to raising my sister and me with this same passionate, personal faith.

She was very committed to living by the Bible's teaching concerning money. I couldn't have been more than 3 or 4 when she started teaching Adessa and me about tithing and giving. She taught us that everything we had came from God and ultimately belonged to God. We learned from her the importance of living on a budget and avoiding debt whenever possible.

She was very open with us about the fact that she got into trouble with debt when she was very young before she was saved, and she determined after that to avoid using credit cards because she never wanted to repeat those mistakes. Because she was firmly committed to being a stay-at-home mom and having Adessa and me in a Christian school, she lived a very frugal lifestyle.

This was the lifestyle I was raised in, and these were the principles that I was taught. She laid a good foundation for us to build our financial lives.

What we didn't know, and she didn't know, was that our foundation was about to be shaken when we found out that although my dad verbally agreed with the Bible's teaching about money, he had been hiding a secret debt for over ten years.

One day, the day I arrived home from college for the summer of my Junior year, Mom decided to go get the mail. She immediately returned to the house and called my dad at work and said, *"We just got a statement from the bank that says we owe them thousands of dollars. There must be a mistake."*

Knowing he was caught, my dad confessed that the mistake was that we owed over double that amount. She was only reading the first of two statements.

In just a few short minutes, everything in our lives was turned upside down by what society now terms "financial infidelity." Without her knowledge, my dad had been borrowing money for over ten years from a line of credit that was tied to their joint checking account. To this day, we don't know where this money went.

Suddenly, we went from thinking we were debt-free to having a major debt. Worse than that, we had just found out that my dad had more than just a few emotional problems tied to his childhood. Here was a pattern of a decade of lies, betrayal, and deceit. It was devastating.

It was a life-changing day for my entire family, especially me. For the first time in my life, I had to begin learning how to properly handle money.

Until then, I was somewhat spoiled when it came to finances. I bought what I wanted when I wanted it. I also spent money to make myself feel like a big man, easing the feelings of inadequacy I faced because of my physical disability. I used money to buy things to ease the pain of years of undealt-with abuse. I used money to meet my emotional needs deep inside, and, as a result, I didn't handle money maturely or responsibly. It was for me and my enjoyment. Now all of a sudden the money wasn't there, and I had to learn how to handle it. We all did.

You see, my mom decided she wasn't giving up on God, she wasn't giving up on my dad, and she wasn't giving up on our finances. That day, she closed my dad's secret account and moved the entire balance to a simple interest loan at our local bank with a very tight repayment schedule. Then she began studying and learning how to start and manage a budget by God's financial principles. She found a financial pamphlet from CBN called "*A Guide to Financial Freedom,*" and she studied it thoroughly. She prayed and sought the Holy Spirit's guidance. Then step by step, she started following the instructions in the booklet and building our family's first real budget.

Let me tell you, our family never experienced financial freedom like we did when we started living on a budget. Don't get me wrong---it was a tight budget. We were making massive payments on dad's debt. We were only spending money on absolute necessities until the debt was paid off. There were boundaries, but in the boundaries there was a feeling of safety, security and remarkable freedom.

Over, the next few months, she converted our entire financial system onto a Biblically based budget of no debt, budgeting, saving, and financial stewardship.

After the debt was paid off, she continued managing our family budget by God's financial principles. She was dedicated to living within our means, saving money for emergencies, and avoiding debt at all costs. She did an awesome job of repairing our devastated finances and structuring our family budget.

I am so grateful. Because of her openness and accountability with the family budget, my sister and I learned valuable principles about money management. These principles have helped us avoid many financial pitfalls and given us an invaluable blueprint for how to live our financial lives. She trained us in the way we should go, and I am committed to not departing from it.

My sister and I saw the results from living on a budget and also from not living on a budget. We've seen the consequences of following God's principles for money and ignoring them. Now, we've committed ourselves to living by God's financial principles and teaching them to other people. Even today, personally and in our ministry, we are committed to living without debt.

When God called me to do the Mantour Conferences, I was financially able to do it because I didn't owe anyone else money. I could take the risk and do what God called me to do. If I had debt, I wouldn't have been able to do this.

Ok, so that is my story, now let's look at how we can all climb Mt. Debt.

1. Realize Debt is Not a Money Issue, It is a Heart Issue—Appetites.

This seems wrong, but it is true. Money is the currency that takes us into debt, but it isn't the cause of debt. Our decisions and actions to spend more money than we have causes debt. As Dave Ramsey says in The Total Money Makeover, *"Money isn't the problem, you're the problem."* [1]

Debt is a heart issue.

I guarantee you, if you are in debt, having more money would not be the thing that gets you out of debt. As a matter of fact, I would bet if you had more money in your life, you would have more debt, too. Why? Because debt is a heart issue.

One of the first things we had to learn as we put our financial house in order was that we had to learn to curb our appetites for things. One of the biggest areas this involves is moving past our need for instant gratification and beginning to wisely manage and save our money.

We do this by learning to curb our appetites. Because ultimately, it's the appetites in our souls that cause us to spend money rather than save it. Until we deal with the deficiencies causing our appetites, we'll never be able to overcome the problem of deficient funds in our savings accounts and living on a budget.

Let's start by defining what I mean by the word "appetite."

An appetite is something we are hungry for. We have an appetite for food. Some have an appetite for sex, some for power. We sometimes use money as a way to feed the appetites of our souls. We want and want, but nothing satisfies. So we buy and buy and end up in debt.

What causes us to have appetites? Some people have "appetites" from deep needs in the soul that were never met. They think that filling their appetites through instant gratification will fill their emotional needs.

Some appetites come from trying to prove to someone else that we are better than them. So we buy things to prove we are as good as or better than they are.

Some allow appetites to take the place of God. Things are used to fill the void only God can fill. But things cost money, and usually money we don't have.

Some have appetites as adults because they grew up poor and resolved to never be poor again. So they work more and more to buy more and more. They live extravagantly and usually in debt.

There are all kinds of unfulfilled needs that each one of us has in our souls because we live in an imperfect world and were raised by imperfect people. This is all a part of life.

We spend money we don't have to fill our emotional needs when what we should be doing is allowing God to heal and fill our emotional needs and using common sense to manage our money.

One of the keys to getting your financial house in order is first realizing how your emotional needs and appetites are affecting your spending habits.

How do we do this?

First, we need to start with prayer.

We need to ask the Holy Spirit to show us what our appetites are and what emotional needs those appetites are trying to fill. A good place to start is by asking yourself, *"Were you poor growing up and did others make fun of you?"* Appetites can drive us to buy things we think we missed growing up. We convince ourselves we need them.

After you've looked at your past, you need to look at your present. Ask yourself some questions like:

• What are my appetites?

• What do I live for?

• What consumes my time?

• What do I have desires for in life? Are they for God? This world? Money? Clothes? Sports? TV? Cars? What?

• What do I hunger and thirst for deep inside my soul?

Once we know the answers to these questions, we will start to recognize our appetites---the emotional issues screaming, *"Feed me, or I'll die!"*

Another thing we can ask ourselves is, *"When do my appetites cause me to spend money?"*

* Do you buy to feel powerful?

* Do you spend money when you're bored?

* Do you buy new expensive "toys" you can't afford to prove your manhood?

* Are you trying to buy your wife's love or your children's love?

You need to recognize how your appetites affect your behavior.

Next, you need to confess your appetites to God.

> *Whoever conceals their sins does not prosper, but the one who confesses and renounces them finds mercy. -Proverbs 28:13 (NIV)*

Ask God to forgive you. Ask Him to forgive you for putting your cravings first in your life before Him.

Then comes the practical part.

Change your mind and lifestyle by reading the Bible and obeying what it says. Ask God to lead you in your new financial journey to freedom.

You see, to keep yourself from sinking into debt, you must stop letting your appetites control your money and you need to start controlling your money according to God's principles.

2. Learn God's Principles for Handling Money.

Did you know that God has given us more than 2,350 verses in the Bible to instruct us on how to manage our money, assets, and resources? In fact, the topic of money is second only to the topic of love in the Bible. Jesus said more about money and possessions than almost any other subject, dedicating over two-thirds of His parables to the subject. If God thinks any topic is that important---then we, as Christians, need to think it is important, too, and be obedient to His commands about it.

So what are God's principles to help us conquer debt?

3. Realize Debt is Not Normal.

The world lies to us and says debt is normal. It says we need to have a good credit score, and that we can't live without credit cards. But it isn't true. It isn't Biblical.

The first step toward changing your attitude about debt is realizing that debt is not normal, it is not healthy, and it is not God's will for Christians to have consumer debt. Although debt is never strictly forbidden in the Bible, it is strongly discouraged and viewed as an unwise way to live.

Again, in Proverbs 22:7 it says, *"The rich rule over the poor, and the borrower is slave to the lender."*

The Bible doesn't pull any punches about debt. It doesn't pretend that it's any more normal to be in debt than it is to be in slavery. If you are in debt to a bank, a credit card agency, a person, or even the government, you work for them until the debt is paid back. Your personal freedom is limited by the fact that you owe money. Also, like we discussed in the beginning, your spiritual freedom is limited by debt.

Proverbs 6 says, *"My child, if you have put up security for a friend's debt or agreed to guarantee the debt of a stranger—if you have trapped yourself by your agreement and are caught by what you said—follow my advice and save yourself, for you have placed yourself at your friend's mercy.*

Now swallow your pride; go and beg to have your name erased. Don't put it off; do it now! Don't rest until you do it. Save yourself like a gazelle escaping from a hunter, like a bird fleeing from a net." (NLT)

Notice, that the Bible doesn't consider getting out of debt optional. It considers it urgent. It basically says, *"Wake up. Do everything necessary to get out of the bondage you've gotten yourself into.*

Go to the point of exhaustion to free yourself before your debt destroys you! Don't ignore it! Don't pretend it doesn't exist! Get up and do something about it!"

If you are a Christian who believes that the Bible is the inspired Word of God meant to be obeyed, then this is the attitude that you need to adopt concerning your debt. You need to start doing everything you can to eliminate it and live in financial freedom--- NOW!

Here's where we start getting practical.

James 2:17-18 says, *"In the same way, faith by itself, if it is not accompanied by action, is dead." (NIV)*

When it comes to the topic of obeying the Bible and freeing ourselves from the bondage of debt, it isn't enough to say, *"We believe this is the right thing to do."* We need to do it! Here are some practical steps you can take to start overcoming your debt.

4. Stop Creating Debt.

It's time to stop spending and stop charging. Adopt the habit of spending only cash. If you don't have the cash to purchase something, then you don't really need it. Cut up the credit cards, close the line of credit at the bank, do whatever you need to do to stop adding to your debt today!

The biggest risk to using credit cards is sinking in debt and losing everything you worked hard to accomplish. Do you know what the biggest risk to only using cash is? Paper cuts!

The biggest risk to using credit cards is sinking in debt and losing everything you worked hard to accomplish. Do you know what the biggest risk to only using cash is? Paper cuts!

5. Take a Realistic View of Your Current Debt.

It's time to take a realistic look at your debt and find out exactly how much you owe. For this to work, you will need to include everything: mortgage payments, car payments, credit cards, consumer loans, school loans, home equity loans---everything. Write the full amount of each loan on a piece of paper, and then add it all together. This is the debt burden you are carrying.

6. Devise a Plan to Start Paying Off Your Debt.

In *The Total Money Makeover*, Dave Ramsey teaches that you make a list of all your debts, from smallest to largest, and then you pay off the smallest first while making minimum payments on the largest. Then when one is paid, you add what you were paying to the next loan on the list until is it paid and so on and so forth. This is a good method because the constant paying off of bills gives a tangible victory and will encourage you to go forward...for someone like me who lives and dies to cross things off a list, this would work fabulously.

As you're creating your debt elimination plan, don't forget to seek the advice of the Holy Spirit. James 1:5 says, *"If you don't know what you're doing, pray to the Father. He loves to help. You'll get his help, and won't be condescended to when you ask for it. Ask boldly, believing, without a second thought."* (The Message)

Remember, He knows your heart, your financial situation, and your future better than anyone. One of His chief roles is to be our Counselor and to reveal truth. Although it is important to seek godly counsel, this must be balanced with a heart that is willing to listen and obey the voice of the Holy Spirit as He leads us.

7. Make Debt Repayment A Top Priority.

Ultimately, you can make all the plans you want, but until you make sticking to your plan a top priority, your debt problem won't be solved.

It wouldn't be fair if I didn't tell you the truth about deciding to eliminate debt from your life. It is going to cost you. Your lifestyle is going to change dramatically---not forever---just until the debt is paid.

Our family basically stopped living until our debt was paid off.

We didn't buy anything that wasn't an absolute necessity. Our budget included paying our bills, buying food and necessities, and paying off our debt. There was no eating out. We stopped buying. The idea of a vacation or any entertainment was out of the question. All money that didn't pay bills was directed toward debt repayment. Dave Ramsey says in The Total Money Makeover that our attitude must be *"to the exclusion of virtually everything else, I am getting out of debt!"*[1]

Not only did we stop spending, but we started selling. We sold anything and everything we didn't need and used this money toward the debt. Tom Rees, the PennDel District's Men's Ministry Director, has a saying that he uses; I think it originated from Dave Ramsey, but he says, *"Sell so much stuff that your kids think they are next!"*

The important thing to remember while you're going through this is that it is only for a certain time in your life. It will not be permanent. If you stop using credit, develop a plan, and commit yourself to sticking to it, there will come a day when your debt will be paid in full. After that happens, you will be able to start living normally again---not overspending, but living normally.

Although I have to warn you, it will be a new normal. It will be normal without the worry, stress, guilt, and fear that accompany debt. Along the way, you'll have picked up some new spending habits which will help you look at money more realistically, live a little less materialistically, and teach you that you can be happy with less. You will never regret it!

Dave Ramsey says, *"If you will live like no one else, later you can live like no one else."*[1]

The final thing we are going to look at is the need to live on a budget.

8. Create a Budget and Stick to It!

The best way to establish financial accountability is to have a budget. Not having a budget is not an option if you want to climb Mt. Debt.

John Maxwell said, *"A budget is people telling their money where to go instead of wondering where it went."* [2]

Dave Ramsey said, *"You have to make your money behave, and a written plan (a budget) is the whip and chair for the money tamer."* [3]

Jesus said, *"But don't begin until you count the cost. For who would begin construction of a building without first calculating the cost to see if there is enough money to finish it?"* -Luke 14:28 (NLV)

You might be asking, *"How can I start living on a budget?"*

Crown Ministries is an excellent place to find information about budgeting. They have a variety of resources that will teach you how to start a budget. They will help you find a method of budgeting that will work in your life. Dave Ramsey also offers a variety of books and resources to help you get started.

Of course, budgeting is only beneficial when you stop thinking about it and reading about it and start doing it.

Don't forget to include the Holy Spirit in your budgeting process.

Pray and ask Him for wisdom, guidance, and self-control as you begin this new adventure.

James 1:5 says, *"If any of you lacks wisdom, you should ask God, who gives generously to all without finding fault, and it will be given to you."* (NIV)

So pray and ask God to give you all the wisdom and help you need on this great adventure of learning to become a good steward of all God's given you.

You can conquer Mt. Debt. You can live in financial freedom. It is possible. God can help you climb this mountain if you are willing to make changes and work to conquer it.

Dear Heavenly Father,

Please forgive me for allowing my finances to be consumed with debt. Help me to work with the Holy Spirit to conquer this debt.

Father forgive me for allowing my appetites to get so out of control, causing me to live beyond my means. Help me to start using money to supply for my family's needs, not as a way to heal my emotional needs.

Help me to start a budget and stick with it. Give me the perseverance to conquer Mt. Debt and live in the freedom you desire for my finances. In Jesus' name, Amen.

Group Study Questions:

1. This chapter says: *"Money and numbers aren't the problems...our actions, attitudes, and spending habits are the problem."* What does this mean?

2. What appetite do you have that contributes to your debt?

3. When do your appetites cause you to spend money?

4. How does God feel about debt?

5. Do you live on a budget? If not, why? Will you commit to developing a budget?

6. After reading this chapter, what is one thing you will put into practice or one thing you will change in your life?

7. How can we, as a group, help you do this?

–Chapter Eleven–

Mt. Grief

I'll never forget that day, no matter how hard I try not to remember it. Being totally honest with you, this is by far the hardest chapter in this book to write, because I don't like going back to this day. It was March 12, just one day after her spiritual birthday, when my mom went to be with Jesus.

Even though she'd struggled with serious health issues for years, her actual passing to Heaven came as a complete surprise.

It was a dark and very stormy Friday night with heavy rain and even heavier wind. We had spent the morning running errands, and in the afternoon I took my mom's car to the garage to get new brakes. After dinner, Mom, Adessa, and I were in the living room laughing and watching TV when she said she had pain. Adessa and I followed as she stood up and walked to her bedroom, where she collapsed into Adessa's arms. I grabbed the phone and dialed 911. Within less than a minute, her body stopped struggling as she went into Jesus' arms.

Soon the ambulance arrived; they quickly hurried us out of the room. They did all they could to work on her, but the coroner later confirmed that she died at home. Still, they took her in the ambulance to the hospital.

Just as the ambulance was preparing to leave, my dad arrived home from work. The three of us piled into the car to follow the ambulance to the hospital forty minutes away.

I remember about ten minutes into the drive, the ambulance pulled over and stopped. I was crying uncontrollably, praying for God to intervene, but Adessa said she knew mom was gone. When we arrived at the hospital, the doctor confirmed that she had passed away.

It was the hardest, scariest, most devastating night of my life.

I'd lost my mom, my mentor, and my closest companion. Still, standing in the hospital room all I could feel was pain, anger, and fear of what was to come. But I knew I had to be strong, take care of Adessa, and call our relatives to let them know what had happened. In that night, I grew up fast.

I honestly don't know what we would have done if it wasn't for our close friend and chiropractor who drove over two hours in horrendous weather to meet us at the hospital and drive us home. Knowing what was going on with my dad, he knew we had no idea how he'd react in his instability. He drove us home and stayed with us until the relatives arrived. He even cleaned up the mess the medics left so that we wouldn't have to see it and did our dishes before the relatives came. I'll always be grateful to this man of God who was there on the day we needed him most.

The next few days seemed like a blur of shock and pain. We had to pick out clothes for her to be buried in and plan the funeral. It was so hard making decisions in the midst of all the pain. My dad was no help at all, and Adessa was completely devastated, so I ended up making a majority of the plans. I was trying to be the strong one and take care of my sister. But as I walked the funeral director out and handed him the clothes for my mom to be buried in, I broke. Alone in our entryway, I sat down and sobbed like I never cried before.

Soon the house was filled with relatives. I remember thinking,

"You can't all sit on our furniture wearing perfume, you'll ruin it and make it impossible for Mom to live in her own house because of her allergies."

Then I'd remember that she wasn't coming back, and another wave of grief would hit me all over again.

On the day of the funeral, the Holy Spirit gave Adessa and me unbelievable strength to speak at the service. Adessa said some things about my mom and spoke to her relatives, and I gave a salvation message---ironically, from an article my mom had written for our online ministry a few weeks before. We knew that Mom would want nothing more than for everyone she loved to hear about Jesus and have the opportunity to go to Heaven with her, so that's what we did.

After the funeral was over, the grieving finally began.

The next few days and weeks and months were filled with incredible grief and pain. It was so hard losing someone I had finally had a restored relationship with, was so close to, loved so much, and spent so much time with. My heart was absolutely broken.

The following months were so hard. Everywhere we went, something would remind me of Mom and a wave of grief would come over me. Our entire lives had revolved around taking care of my mom the past few years and protecting her from my dad's abuse. We had given up everything to do this, and now we literally had to not only deal with grief, but also build a new life for ourselves. During this time, life became a series of putting one foot in front of the other and making it through the grieving process.

Day by day we continued moving forward in pain and through the pain. Of all the difficult things we went through, this was by far the hardest. I'm grateful I didn't have to go through it alone, but Adessa was there to walk it with me.

Moment by moment, sometimes breath by breath, God was with us---comforting, guiding, and leading us through the valley of the shadow of death.

Slowly we climbed Mt. Grief. It was one of the hardest mountains to climb. But God helped us through this time.

Grief can absolutely cripple us. People experience grief in many different ways:

- Loss of a parent

- Loss of a child

- Loss of loved ones

- The end of a friendship

- Divorce

- Seeing your children walk away from God

- Loss of a job

On and on the list goes of ways grief can enter our lives. I have seen way too many people be crippled by grief. They stay cemented to the foot of Mt. Grief, unable to move forward.

Adessa and I love to watch Christmas movies. I am a HUGE Christmas guy. One of Adessa's favorite movies is a Hallmark movie (yes I watch Hallmark Christmas movies, and no you can't have my man card!) that has a character in it who leaves her house decorated and lights turned on all year long. Jokes are made about this woman throughout the movie, but at the end we learn why she had Christmas year-round. She tells someone that the man she loved had introduced her to his fiancé on Christmas Eve over twenty years ago, and for her, the loss crippled her. Her grief made her stay at Christmas Eve forever.

Grief has a way of stopping us cold. Because of the pain, we stay where we are, unable to handle moving forward. I know firsthand.

You see, after my mom passed away, Adessa and I were forced to start over and start a new life. We had to find friends, find a support system, and grow our ministry. We went from being bloggers while we took care of mom and kept dad from abusing her to full-time ministers. We spent every ounce of our energy and strength doing this. We were able, with God's help to start over with our "careers." But we didn't move forward with our lives.

This past Christmas season God started pointing this out to me. As the holidays rolled in, we had more time off the road and at home. During this time, the Holy Spirit decided to do a little spiritual surgery on my heart to deal with some scar tissue from the grief that wasn't healed properly in my life. What do I mean?

Well, the best way to sum it up would be to apply it to Christmas. When I was a kid and a young adult, I LOVED Christmas. I was Mr. Christmas, wearing my Santa hat, listening to Christmas music, decorating anything and everything that moved. I was Buddy the Elf, Clark Griswold, and Tim "The Toolman" Taylor rolled into one--- you get the idea. But then our family started down the decade long, very dark season full of hurt, pain, deeper levels of abuse...just a really hard, painful time. Things like Christmas took a backseat as we dealt with the daily torment we were living in.

Then there was the first Christmas after my mom died. Full of grief and sorrow, we didn't really even try to celebrate Christmas. The next few years were similar, each year adding a little bit more Christmas activity but still not embracing the holiday. To avoid the pain, I would usually work all day on Christmas...better to be busy than to feel the grief.

Two years ago, my mentor pretty much demanded we take off work for Christmas. Man, was I mad at him! But I submitted, and we reintroduced Christmas into our lives. For the first time in at least fifteen years, we put up a tree. We decorated the inside of our house, and we bought each other presents. I won't lie, it was hard, but I forced myself to celebrate Christmas...and some healing began to take place!

Then, last year, we fully embraced Christmas. We watched cheesy Hallmark movies, Christmas music rang through our house, the whole nine yards. For the first time in a long time, the old Jamie was back...and I liked having him around again!

Now don't think this was just a holiday nostalgia or the script for another cheesy Hallmark film...it wasn't really about Christmas. The Holy Spirit began to show me that over the years, through all the grief, loss, abuse, hurt, pain, and horror our lives went through, I had erected a wall around my heart.

Sure, I was great at dreaming when it came to ministry! I love to dream and allow the Holy Spirit to plant visions and dreams of how to use our ministry to reach more men....I am good at that. But dreaming in my personal life...not so much. No one, nothing, was going to hurt me again! I was done feeling, and I was definitely done dreaming; personal disappointment hurt too much! I was stuck knee-deep in the mud surrounding Mt. Grief.

But this December, the Holy Spirit started showing me that this was no way to live! He showed me my identity can't be derived from what I do; it had to come from him. He opened my eyes to see that I had stopped doing the one thing people need to have hope...dreaming.

It reminded me of the Batman movie, *The Dark Knight Rises*, one of my favorites! In that movie, Bane throws Bruce Wayne into the pit with no ceiling and no way to escape. He says, *"There's a reason why this prison is the worst hell on earth... Hope. Every man who has ventured here over the centuries has looked up to the light and imagined climbing to freedom. So easy... So simple... And like shipwrecked men turning to sea water from uncontrollable thirst, many have died trying. I learned here that there can be no true despair without hope."*[1]

Grief and pain caused me to give up on hope, because it hurt too badly. But my Heavenly Father showed me that this was wrong. I had to begin hoping again, feeling again, allowing myself to be excited again. I had to start living again and enjoying life.

He has given me a really good life, and I am living my dream! It is okay to be happy. It is okay to take time to have fun. I need to begin enjoying my personal life as much as I do my ministry life.

Grief had caused me to stop living. It caused me to stop dreaming. I needed to dream again! I was always a born dreamer, but the hurt and pain of unrealized dreams and grief over the years caused me to stop dreaming. But I have come to realize this self-protection mechanism has been robbing life from me. Enough was enough; it was time to live again! It was time to dream again!

I share this to encourage you that you can conquer grief that is crippling your life. There is hope for you. Don't cut off your heart and emotions to ease the pain. It doesn't ease it, it just buries it. And slowly, it kills your spirit. You've stayed at Mt. Grief too long!

Don't cut off your heart and emotions to ease the pain. It doesn't ease it, it just buries it. And slowly, it kills your spirit. You've stayed at Mt. Grief too long!

I want to share with you some things we learned about grief, and how you can climb this mountain!

1. Only You Know How You Need to Grieve.

We live in a world that tries to put grief into a box. *"This is how you should feel when you lose...."*

What I've learned is that grief is different for everyone depending on your personality and your relationship with the person you've lost.

One of the hardest things for me going through this process was that people seemed to feel I was overreacting to the loss of a parent. It wasn't as if I had lost a spouse or a child.

Yet in my situation, Mom and I were extremely close, despite the years where my dad had driven us apart. We had reestablished a relationship and become very, very close. I remember one of the people in town saying, *"I've never seen a family as close as yours....we hardly ever saw one of you that we didn't see all three,"* referring to Mom, Adessa and me. So my grief didn't fit into the "parent/child" grief box.

By going through this I've learned that it's wrong to tell someone how they should feel or how deeply they should hurt. If you're going through grief, you shouldn't feel guilty if you feel more or less than people think you should. Everyone grieves in their own way, at their own pace, and in their own time. If you know someone who is going through grief, minister to them where they are….don't try to fit them into a box of where you think they should be.

One of the most helpful pieces of advice came from a lady who'd been through a tragedy herself. She said, *"Things are going to be hard for a few months. Your heart is going to hurt and life will be difficult for awhile. But in time things will get better. In six months, it won't hurt as bad as it does now. The first holidays will be difficult, but each one will get better. Let yourself feel the pain now, and don't push yourself to rush through it, but know that things will get better."* Her words released me from the pressure to feel better quickly, but they also offered me hope.

2. You Can't Hurry Grief.

Even more than the pressure to grieve less deeply, one of the hardest things for me was dealing with people who didn't think I was grieving fast enough. There was one couple in particular who really pushed the attitude that our mom was happy in Heaven, so we needed to move on. So much so that just hours after the funeral they were encouraging us to do things that there was no way on earth I was prepared to do.

As the months went on they continued to offer "help" in the form of pushing us into things we weren't ready to handle. I remember they were really big on the "helping others will heal your heart theory." To a degree they were right. We learned this lesson during our first Thanksgiving/Christmas without Mom. However, I couldn't help others weeks after she passed…I was still hurting too much at that point.

Eventually, we had to stop giving these well-meaning people a voice in our pain. Instead, we learned to follow the leading of the Holy Spirit who led us step by step through the grieving process. Because He knew the whole situation we were walking through, He knew when we needed to move forward and in what direction. When I stopped listening to people's opinions and instead chose to follow His timing, I felt much less pressure and stress, and He gave us the strength to meet every challenge and move forward with Him.

3. Sometimes You Need a Little Help from God's People.

I know this sounds like it goes against the last point, but it doesn't. The truth is, that while you can't let other people tell you how to grieve, you also can't walk through grief alone.

One of the things that really helped us was the counsel of a local Assemblies of God pastor who helped us work through our grief and restart our new life. As he listened and offered advice, we were able to see things from a perspective that wasn't clouded with grief. That helped us make wiser decisions as we moved forward.

Perhaps you don't feel you need the help of a counselor. At least make sure to surround yourself with a few trusted friends who will listen to you and lend you a shoulder to cry on. Looking back, I can see that one of the things that helped me the most through this process was having a sister who would just listen to me talk and cry. Together we were there for each other so that neither of us felt alone.

4. Don't Make Any Decisions the First Year.

We received this advice from people who had been through the grieving process, and we found it very helpful. That's why I'd encourage anyone who is grieving to avoid making any big decisions that will affect your life drastically right away. Looking back, I can see that really the first two years most of my decisions were clouded by pain and grief. Although they were the right choices for those times, after we started to heal and become ourselves again, we felt led to make changes and different choices.

Even though it may feel like you have to decide everything right now...you don't. Give yourself some time, focus on healing, and the Holy Spirit will help you make the right decisions at the right time.

5. Grief is More of a Cycle.

Loving to study psychology, I went into the grieving process with a lot of knowledge about the Five Stages of Grieving: Denial, Bargaining, Anger, Depression, and Resolve.

However, in my own personal experience, I didn't find these stages to be so much a 1, 2, 3, 4, 5 step process as much as a cycle. I could feel any one at any time, sometimes all at the same time.

In my experience, grief comes more in waves. Good days are mixed with bad days. At any moment, a song, a word, something you smell or hear can trigger your grief.

Smell was a big trigger for me...whenever I smelled something that would have been an allergen for my mom, my brain would trigger "Panic."

Holidays brought on lots of waves of grief and emotions.

Whatever the trigger, in a moment, I could feel anger, sadness, depression, or even shock all over again. The good thing about waves is that they come and they pass...grief is like that...it comes, you feel it, and then you get back up and keep moving forward again.

And then there's the stage that no one talks about in the Five Stages of Grief.

5. Don't Get Stuck in Guilt.

Years ago I heard a quote that said, *"Only the dead feel no guilt."*

I thought of it many times during my grieving process.

From talking with other people I've learned that although it's not often mentioned, guilt is a big part of the grieving process.

• "I wish I would have been there..."

• "Maybe if I'd have done more..."

- "What if I'd done something differently...."

- "If I'd have gotten to the doctors faster...."

- "Could I have made them happier while they were here..."

All of these questions and more race through your mind when you're grieving. Maybe it's part of the bargaining process that our mind has to go through. I know I went over them a thousand times in my head.

The truth is that death is a part of life. It's one of the hardest parts because we generally can't control it.

Pastor Jim Cymbala from Brooklyn Tabernacle recently said on Facebook, *"No matter what is happening around you, as a Christian you will not die one second before God wants to take you home."*

This is hard for us to accept. Somehow we want to believe that we can control things and when the uncontrollable happens, we blame ourselves.

We need to resurrender our will to God's Divine will and accept that He controls even the things that we do not understand.

If you are going through this today, let me first assure you that this is a normal default that your brain goes through as you're going through the grieving process. Just because you feel guilty doesn't mean you are or that you had any control over the situation.

What I've found is that the only way to overcome this particular obstacle is confession. Talk to Jesus about how you feel. Talk to a trusted friend. Talking gets it out of your system and off of your mind. Every once in a while a piece of truth that you hear will seep into your grieving heart and set you free from some of the things you believe.

Over time, you will, like I did, come to the place where you accept that you cannot control life and death. These things must be left in God's hands. As human beings, we need to surrender our will to the Divine will and accept that He controls even the things that we do not understand.

As you work toward this goal, you'll be able to move beyond guilt and closer to healing and acceptance. You will climb Mt. Grief!

6. Jesus Can Handle Your Grief.

An excellent example of this is Mary and Martha. In John 11, we read the story of the death of their brother, Lazarus. Although they called Jesus to come and heal Lazarus while he was still alive, Jesus delayed his arrival until after Lazarus had passed away.

When Jesus finally did arrive on the scene, Mary and Martha were drowning in grief.

Both of them, in their own way, unloaded all of their grief on Jesus basically saying, *"This is YOUR fault---if you'd have come, this wouldn't have happened."*

They were filled with disappointment—not unbelief—disappointment. They were shocked at what happened. They were confused. They were grieving.

How did Jesus respond to these two hurting women? John 11:33-35 tell us:

> *When Jesus saw her weeping, and the Jews who had come along with her also weeping, he was deeply moved in spirit and troubled. "Where have you laid him?" he asked.*
>
> *"Come and see, Lord," they replied.*
>
> *Jesus wept.*

Jesus was moved by their heartache. He identified with their pain. He didn't say, *"Come on, get a grip. This is what God wanted."*

No, He cried with them. He comforted them. He was moved by their agony. He hurt because He saw the emotional pain these women were suffering.

Jesus wasn't offended by their questions.

He didn't call their words a sin.

He understood that they were shocked and disappointed. Even though He knew that this was all a part of God's plan, He understood that they didn't know God's plan.

He didn't criticize or judge them.

He wasn't harsh with them. Rather, He cried because He understood how difficult it was for these women to live through the plans that God had orchestrated.

His heart went out to them. His love for Mary and Martha caused Him to weep. Because He is the same yesterday, today, and forever, this same Jesus hurts for you when you are grieving. (Hebrews 13:8) Although He knows the why's and the outcomes, His heart goes out to you in your time of pain.

Hebrews 4:15-16 says:

> *We don't have a priest who is out of touch with our reality. He's been through weakness and testing, experienced it all—all but the sin. So let's walk right up to him and get what he is so ready to give. Take the mercy, accept the help. (The Message)*

The Bible even says that Jesus prays for us. (Hebrew 7:25) Because He came to earth and experienced humanity, He is able to identify with our suffering. From that understanding, He intercedes for us to the Heavenly Father.

Remember, Jesus experienced all kinds of pain and suffering while He was on earth. Among these was the pain of losing His earthly father, Joseph.

He understands the feelings and emotions that accompany grief when tragedies strike and disappointments occur.

He isn't offended by angry, painful questions of "*Why? How could you let this happen?*"

He just says, "*Come to me. Tell me how you feel. Let it all out. I understand that you are hurting.*"

Like He was with Mary and Martha, He wants to be there with you. Although I can't promise that you will get a miracle like Mary and Martha did, I can promise that Jesus will be there for you to help you every step of the way. He will help you walk through every step of the grieving process, and He will help you start a new life. He will help you climb Mt. Grief.

I know because that's what He did for Adessa and me. He'll do the same for you.

7. In Grief, We Need to Run Toward God, Not Away From Him.

When we experience loss and are faced with the challenge of starting over, whether it be loss of a loved one, loss of a job, or loss of a relationship, this is a choice you make over and over again.

It's not always easy because part of you wants to run away from God because you are angry that He allowed this to happen to you. Your heart hurts, and you don't like this difficult time you are walking through.

On the other hand, deep inside, you know that He is the only one who can give you the help and strength you need to get through this time. You need his direction and guidance as you wade through the myriad of decisions you need to make.

One way I was very blessed is that I had the opportunity to watch my mom model someone who turned to God when she was experiencing grief. During her life, I watched her walk through many difficult circumstances.

I saw her grieve over many people that she loved. Some of them didn't even die, they just chose to walk away and reject her. I saw her grieve the loss of those relationships. I was there when she experienced betrayal and tremendous disappointments.

Each time, as she turned the page and started a new chapter in her life, she determined that she would continue to follow God and overcome. She had an unwavering devotion that no matter what happened, she was going through it with God—not without Him. She said she could lose a lot of things in life, but she could never lose her relationship with God. In every trial, she ran toward Him and submitted to His plan for her life.

There were times when her commitment amazed me, because I watched her go through some devastating difficulties. Years later as I walked through my own difficulties, her example inspired me to keep running toward God.

What exactly does this mean?

For me, it meant making time to spend with Him, seeking His direction for my life and His wisdom for the many choices that must be made. To be honest, sometimes those times consisted of me, like Mary and Martha, telling Him how much I hurt or how angry I was about what He chose to bring into my life. Then I asked Him to heal those hurts and give me the strength to go on. During this time I have realized that I desperately need the help only He can give. Like my mom, I have learned to run to Him, not away from Him in my hour of need because it's only in Him that true healing can be found.

8. Commit Your Way to God.

Another part of climbing Mt. Grief is committing yourself to following God's ways.

It's a choice each of us must make individually. Are we willing to place our lives in His hands even without a guaranteed outcome?

I can tell you that God has a plan for your life. Whatever tragedy you are experiencing didn't come as a surprise to God. He will take care of you if you will choose to put your life in His hands and follow His ways.

Trust me, I know how difficult this choice can be. I know it is hard to trust the God who let this tragedy happen to you. Still, He is the only One who has the answers. If we choose to follow Him, to run toward Him and not away from Him, He will help us. It's a choice I had to make, and it's a choice you need to make. This is the only path toward healing and a new life. It is the best direction to choose when you are starting over.

Finally:

9. There is Hope.

Weeping may stay for the night, but rejoicing comes in the morning. - Psalm 30:5 (NIV)

As we're going through the grieving process, we need to remember that this is only a season in our lives.

This is only a season in your life. You will not always be grieving. You will not always be starting over in life. Eventually, your new life will become your normal life.

You will not always be grieving. You will not always be starting over in life.

Eventually, your new life will become your normal life.

Right now if you are in a place of grief and starting over, you feel like the world has come to an end. It's hard enough to get through a day, let alone think about God taking care of the future. On the other hand, you are probably scared to death about the future and wondering if you will ever feel anything but grief again.

I know because I felt this way some days.

It's in those days that we need to believe God's Word and not our own feelings.

The Bible says in Isaiah 61 that Jesus will:

Comfort all who mourn, and provide for those who grieve in Zion, to bestow on them a crown of beauty instead of ashes, the oil of gladness instead of mourning, and a garment of praise instead of a spirit of despair. (NIV)

Matthew 5:4 says: *"Blessed are those who mourn, for they will be comforted." (NIV)*

Ecclesiastes 3:1, 4 says, *"There is a time for everything and a season for every activity under Heaven. A time to weep and a time to laugh. A time to mourn and a time to dance." (NIV)*

This is basically what I experienced earlier when God told me it was time to live and enjoy life again.

I don't mean to sound insensitive at all, because I know how you feel, but I want to encourage you that this isn't forever.

How do I know this?

Three years ago, my sister and I had the opportunity to go to the beach while Adessa spoke at a ministry event. Heading into our evening at the beach, I was beyond excited.

In the end, it didn't disappoint. It was absolutely beautiful—and relaxing—and absolutely fun. I'm sure our friends on social media thought we were ridiculous with all of the pictures we shared—but for us, those few hours of fun at the beach was something that we hadn't experienced in almost fifteen years. And we enjoyed every single minute of it!!!

Of course, this wasn't the first time we'd been to the ocean in fifteen years—it was just the first time we'd enjoyed it.

The truth is that the very last time I was at the beach was just a few short weeks after my mom had gone to be with Jesus. It was Mother's Day weekend (the first without her), and we tried to escape the pain by getting away. As anyone who has gone through deep grief understands, there is no escaping grief—it follows you wherever you go.

Well, it was only a few weeks after she passed away that we decided to go to the beach and stay in a hotel for the first time in over ten years. As soon as I walked into the hotel room and smelled the chemicals they used to clean it, my radar went off and my brain recognized "Danger."

Only there was no more danger because my mom wasn't there. Immediately, I was overcome with intense grief.

It was the most awful vacation ever, and we went back home less than twenty-four hours after we had arrived. Years later, as we were driving toward the ocean, I couldn't help but remember that trip from years ago. Only this time, that's all I did—remember.

There was no pain.

No intense grief.

Even though I remembered my mom when we were at the ocean or purchasing salt water taffy from her favorite candy store, this time the grief was replaced by joy and happy memories of days gone by.

In that moment, I realized something: the grief was gone. The pain had healed. I had climbed Mt. Grief!

It really is true: weeping may endure for a night, but joy comes in the morning.

As I laughed and had fun at the beach, took silly selfies, ate salt water taffy, and watched the waves, I stood as a testimony to anyone who is grieving that there is hope. Grief does not last forever.

Healing comes. Joy returns. The pain fades and the fond memories will return.

Today, if you find yourself grieving, I want to encourage you: you will make it. This will not last forever.

No, I'm not diminishing your hurt or the fact that you can't see past the pain right now. I'm just telling you as someone who's been there and walked through it, that you will have brighter days again. If you allow Him, God will heal your pain and restore your soul.

This season of grief is only a season. Like all seasons, it will change.

Whether you're grieving the loss of a loved one, a relationship, a hope or dream, a job or any loss, I want to encourage you today that you are going to be okay.

Keep walking forward, keep trusting Jesus, and know that your heart will heal, and you will find joy again.

I know because I did. Even though years ago, I couldn't imagine being happy and pain-free again, I can now stand as a testimony that through Jesus, you can heal. You can forgive. You can move forward, and you will find joy again.

Dear Heavenly Father,

You know the feeling of grief and loss I am drowning in. I feel so lost, alone, and hopeless. But I don't want to stay stuck at Mt. Grief forever.

Help me to not bury my grief, but help me work through the grief so I can move on from this mountain. Help me to turn to You and trust You through the grief, not to push You away. Bring godly friends into my life to help me through.

I don't want to stay stuck in my grief forever. Help me work through the grief and come through to the other side. In Jesus' name, Amen.

GROUP STUDY QUESTIONS:

1. What has caused grief in your life?

2. How can we balance not avoiding grief with not staying at Mt. Grief for too long?

3. How can guilt trap us in grief?

4. How can you run towards God during times of grief?

5. After reading this chapter, what is one thing you will put into practice or one thing you will change in your life?

6. How can we, as a group, help you do this?

-CHAPTER TWELVE-

MT. PORN

But this time, Lord you gave me a mountain, A mountain you
know I may never climb,
It isn't just a hill any longer, You gave me a mountain this time.[1]

I was mesmerized. The coal black hair. The shiny sequence jumpsuits. The deep voice full of conviction and passion. What was I watching?

Elvis Presley's 1972 *Aloha From Hawaii Via Satellite* concert! A music spectacular!!

Of course, it wasn't the live performance. (I am not that old!) It was a VHS tape rented from Blockbuster. (If you're too young to know what Blockbuster is, then Google is your friend.)

My mom LOVED Elvis, and her love was passed on to me. My mom was a very strict Christian woman, and she was VERY strict on the TV shows and music we watched and listened to growing up. But the one exception was Elvis. She allowed us to watch Elvis' movies when they were on TV. Many a summer morning was spent watching silly Elvis flicks before heading to the pool in the afternoon.

But this concert rental was special. We rarely rented videos, I can really only think of four or five times we did it. One of those times was this Elvis Live Concert.

I will never forget the first time I heard Elvis sing the song referenced above. Maybe it was the big drums in it or the way Elvis sang it with such passion, but I was mesmerized.

As I have been thinking about the theme of conquering our mountains, my mind turned to a HUGE mountain that many men have standing right in front of them: pornography. Too many men, believers included, are trapped in pornography and, like Elvis, are screaming, *"This is a mountain I can't climb!"*

I know this is true. I have been there. Pornography was a major struggle for me in my late teens and college years.

As I said earlier in this chapter, my mom was VERY VERY strict in what she would allow us to watch growing up. She made sure she protected her children from the perversion that was beginning to really dominate our society. As a child, I was very innocent and pure.

I remember the first time I saw pornography. I was about eight or nine and my father and I were helping a friend in his garage. When I walked into the garage, there were pictures of naked women all over the walls.

I was stunned. Even more than that, I was heartbroken.

I made the decision in my young heart that I didn't want to see a naked woman until my wedding night. That dream was over. Stunned, I turned to my dad for comfort and reassurance only to have him tell me to get over it. He said it was no big deal.

As I grew through my teenage years, I was still very naive when it came to sex. I remember in the high school locker room after gym class hearing the other guys in my Christian school talk about sex, masturbation, and other such things and having no idea what they were talking about. Because I already struggled with feeling like a real man or good enough because of my disability, having this second area where I wasn't like all the other guys really affected me. I felt so inadequate and so different. At the time, I didn't realize it was a good difference...all I knew was that I wasn't like everyone else.

To be more "normal" (according to the world), I started watching things I shouldn't have watched. It started with watching people on TV make out, and, as I grew older, it grew deeper.

When I entered Bible college, I fell into the trap of online pornography. It was sad. I was training to be a minister, and all the while, was trapped in pornography. I can remember leading men's small groups on campus, and then watching pornography on my computer afterwards. I was a mess!

While I never actually followed through with my desires or lost my virginity, I was stuck in the cycle of watching pornography again and again. I wanted to quit, but I ended up failing over and over. It was a mad cycle...watching pornography, repenting, and promising to never do it again. But as the Bible says, I was like a pig returning to it's vomit (Proverbs 26:11) ...I kept going back for more.

Eventually I reached my breaking point. I wanted to be free! I didn't want to be trapped in this cycle any longer. I took action, and God delivered me. What action did I take?

1. I Confessed.

I wanted out of this mad cycle, and the only way I knew to break free was to get out of the darkness and step into the light...meaning, I had to confess the sin to someone.

Thankfully, I had a godly mother to whom I could confess my sin and seek help. Admitting my struggle to her was embarrassing and one of the hardest things I ever did, but it was a life changing moment for me.

I also had a mentor, a professor in college, I could confess my sin to, and he was a source of strength to me as I fought to overcome. I am happy to say that in my early twenties, I was able to overcome and live a pure life before God. I got victory over Mt. Pornography!

This is a HARD step, but a necessary step. If you want to break free from pornography's bondage, you need to find a TRUSTWORTHY, MATURE believer and tell them about your struggle. While humiliating, confessing destroys pornography's strongest grip, being secretive and hidden. The light of confession burns away the darkness of sin.

You need to find a TRUST-WORTHY, MATURE believer and tell them about your struggle... The light of confession burns away the dark sin.

You need to confess the sin to someone and ask them to become your accountability partner. Give them permission to hold you accountable and to be tough on you.

2. Repent.

The next thing I did was to ask God to forgive me for watching pornography and getting trapped in this disgusting cycle. I asked God to forgive me, to purify my mind, and to give me victory.

Why wasn't this Step One? Well, to be honest, I had asked God many times to forgive me, but I kept returning to the dark, secret sin. I had to break the sin's power and expose myself. Then I was able to repent and ask God to forgive me.

The best way to deal a blow to the enemy is to go before God and repent of any and all sexual sins you have committed in the past. Take a sheet of paper and, through the power of the Holy Spirit, identify times you have sinned sexually in the past. Include any TV shows, movies, magazines, video games, thoughts and actions.

Then spend time in prayer confessing these sins to God. Ask Him to forgive you. Ask God to restore your mind to purity and holiness like His. Begin to live a pure and holy life before God.

Repentance is key to overcoming pornography. Why?

Because pornography is sinning against God.

Sure it affects us and our relationships, but it is really a sin against our Heavenly Father.

David understood this. David knew his sin was his fault and was sin against God. Read his confession in Psalms 51:

> *For I know my transgressions, and my sin is always before me.* ***Against you, you only, have I sinned*** *and done what is evil in your sight; so you are right in your verdict and justified when you judge.*
>
> *Surely I was sinful at birth, sinful from the time my mother conceived me. Yet you desired faithfulness even in the womb; you taught me wisdom in that secret place.*
>
> *Cleanse me with hyssop, and I will be clean; wash me, and I will be whiter than snow Let me hear joy and gladness; let the bones you have crushed rejoice. Hide your face from my sin and* ***blot out all my iniquity.***
>
> ***Create in me a pure heart, O God, and renew a steadfast spirit within me. Do not cast me from your presence or take your Holy Spirit from me. Restore to me the joy of your salvation and grant me a willing spirit, to sustain me.*** *(NIV, emphasis added)*

I remember praying these verses to God, and asking Him to forgive me. I recommend you do the same.

3. View Sex the Way God Views Sex.

The third thing I did was figure out why exactly pornography is wrong.

Sounds silly, doesn't it? But in order to kill pornography, I had to realize why pornography was wrong and damaging. I needed a logical argument. This is what I came up with.

God doesn't approve of us having sex in the wrong place and the wrong time. How is pornography sex in the wrong place? Watching pornography isn't really having sex is it? Well, let's look at what Jesus says.

Matthew 5:27-28 says:

> *You have heard that it was said, "You shall not commit adultery." But I tell you that anyone who looks at a woman lustfully has already committed adultery with her in his heart. (NIV)*

Pornography is the same as having sex, it says so right there. Sex is meant for the marriage bed, not a dark room in front of a computer screen. The wrong place is alone in a room with a computer screen.

Sex is meant for the marriage bed, not a dark room in front of a computer screen.

Many men see this as an impossible standard. They feel they have a right to look at a pretty girl and fantasize about her. However, Jesus makes it clear. You don't. If we look at a woman lustfully, if we fantasize about a woman, if we masturbate, it is sin against God. There is no way around it. That is God's rule.

Sex at the wrong time is sex with anyone who isn't your wife, whether you are single or married.

Sex was created to be between a husband and a wife. Having an affair in marriage will damage your relationships. It causes life-changing damage to the spouse and children involved. It hurts co-workers, friends, and churches. It is not just a private act. It kills many relationships and destroys reputations.

If you're single, having sex before marriage will damage your future marriage relationship. God does not condone sex before marriage. He understands all the baggage and garbage this will cause to your future relationship, so us single guys need to abstain from sex and save it for our wedding night.

To have pre-marital sex or an affair is to be anti-family and anti-God. It is cheating on the wife you took a sacred vow with on your wedding day. Single guys, sex before marriage is cheating on your future spouse, it is the same as if you had an affair while married to her.

All that to say, I had to change my thinking about pornography and sex and view it as God views it.

Were these steps hard? Heck yeah!

It was hard, humiliating, and humbling. But it was worth it! I was set free! I am here to tell you today, you can conquer Mt. Pornography! Your prayer needs to become, *"God give me this mountain! Help me overcome my addiction to pornography!"* Then begin to climb!

You see, God will help us; He will give us victory. But we still have to do our part. We have to climb! We have to take action to change through God's power.

I wish I could say that defeating Mt. Pornography is a once and done battle. Getting the victory is a one time event, but you will have to constantly make sure you stay victorious.

The good news is that I have some helpful ways to help you do this.

1. Be Proactive.

We need to take action before the temptation of pornography strikes by identifying the areas of your life that cause you to be tempted to sin sexually.

• Where are you?

• What are you doing?

• What are you feeling?

• What is going on around you?

You have to try and anticipate the weak times when the attack comes so you can build up a defense to overcome. After you identify your triggers, develop a clear battle plan to overcome. Establish steps to take to resist the temptation.

For instance, if your greatest moment of weakness is late at night when you are tired and alone, then use tools like parental controls on TV and internet to block usage late at night. Develop a plan and stick to it!

2. Keep A Short Balance Sheet With God.

In the future, keep a short account with God. Any time even a thought or desire to sin sexually or watch pornography pops up, cast it down in Jesus' name. Confess it and move on, continuing the pursuit of sexual purity.

3. Do a Media Fast.

I know I have suggested this in my other books, but I need to repeat it here because it is such a powerful tool. For one month, do not watch any TV or any movies or play any video games. Instead, take that time and spend it reading the Bible. You will be surprised at the end of the month how little TV your conscience will allow you to watch after renewing your mind.

4. Use All the Tools Available.

The bad thing about technology is the enemy has figured out how to use it for destructive attacks against a man's purity. The good thing about technology is that godly men have learned ways to safeguard against the enemy's attacks.

Lots of tools are available to help God's men. Use your TV's V-chip to block out sexual content from your TV. Have someone else control the password so that you don't give into temptation. The great thing about a V-Chip password is that if you don't know it, you can't use it.

Covenant Eyes is a great internet filter that can be used on your computers, phones, and tablets. It also has an accountability feature that will send a list of what you look at online to a mentor. I highly recommend this product.

Another great option to help keep pornography out of your life is with a CleanRouter. CleanRouter blocks pornography from ever entering your home, church, or business. Instead of installing it on all your devices, it is installed on your network, so any device, whether a smart TV, computer, phone, or tablet that uses your network is protected.

5. Find A Band of Brothers To Hold You Accountable.

Peer pressure is a great weapon when it comes to fighting pornography. We need men around us who we allow total access to, to ask us any questions and hold us accountable whenever they see the need.

Allow your Band of Brothers to see your internet history. Make them friends on your gaming network so they see what games you play. Be an open book to them, allowing no question or topic to be off-limits.

6. Go Commando.

Take whatever steps are necessary to live sexually pure. Jesus said in Matthew 5, *"If your right hand offends you, cut it off."*

He wasn't suggesting self-mutilation. He was saying we are better off getting rid of whatever causes us to sin even if it hurts.

It's better to lose Google temporarily than to lose your soul eternally.

If pornography on the internet causes you to sin, get rid of the internet. While the internet is handy, people got along for centuries without it, and if it causes you to sin, it is better to lose Google temporarily than to lose your soul eternally.

If TV or movies cause you to stumble, cancel your cable and Netflix. Better to miss the latest reality show than to lose your soul.

Do video games cause you to sin? Then sell your system on eBay. Better to not be a gamer than to lose your soul.

7. Read Every Man's Battle and Tactics by Fred Stoeker.

I strongly suggest that all men read these two books by Fred Stoeker. They are excellent teachings to help break the grips of pornography.

8. Seek the Help Of A Christian Counselor.

If you find yourself in a place where you cannot conquer the sexual sins and temptations, no matter what you try, you may be facing a spiritual stronghold in your life. Like I did with my battle with fear, I would recommend seeking out the help of a counselor trained in spiritual warfare to help you break the stronghold.

9. Devour the Word of God.

The Bible says that we need to renew our minds. The best way to do this is through devouring God's Word. When struggling to stay pure in an impure world, we need to read the Word like never before. It is hard to sin sexually while reading the Word of God. It is hard to think impure thoughts while thinking the thoughts of God found in His Word. The best way to conquer impurity is to soak our minds in God's Word.

10. If All Else Fails, Run!

> *Flee from sexual immorality. All other sins a person commits are outside the body, but whoever sins sexually, sins against their own body. -1 Corinthians 6:18 (NIV)*

Whenever the New Testament discusses the subject of sensual temptation, it gives one command: RUN! The Bible does not tell us to reason with it. It tells us to FLEE! We cannot yield to sensuality and pornography if we are running away from it.

Run for your life. Get out of there! If we try to reason with the desire to watch pornography or entertain sexual thoughts, we will give in to them. We won't be able to fight it. This is why God forcefully orders us to run away from it.

This is the one situation where a godly man should not stand up and fight. With all other temptations, we have to nuke them. But not sexual temptation. It is a losing battle. Run with all your might.

These 10 tips are great weapons to use in your battle to break free and stay free of the grip of pornography. I know, firsthand, that freedom is possible. You can leave Mt. Pornography behind you!

Dear Heavenly Father,

Please forgive me for watching pornography and for the resulting sins that come from watching pornography. Cleanse my mind from the damage I have done to it through these sexual sins. Help me to change my behavior in these areas.

Help me to develop a battle plan to overcome these temptations, and help me to be man enough to run when any sexual temptation or desire to watch pornography may come. I want to be a man committed to sexual purity. In Jesus' name, Amen.

NOTE:

Covenant Eyes: You can get one month of protection free if you sign up via the link at our website www.mantourministries.com under "Resources."

Clean Router: You can save 25% if you sign up via the link at our website www.mantourministries.com under the "Resource" tab.

GROUP STUDY QUESTIONS:

1. What are some sexual triggers that people are susceptible to?

2. When are you most vulnerable to sexual temptation?

3. What are several ways of escape you will utilize when you become aware you're being tempted?

4. Why is having an accountability partner important? What are the two most important questions you'd advise an accountability partner to ask you when you meet?

5. What is our role in partnership with the power of the Holy Spirit to gain freedom and transformation? What is the Holy Spirit's role in partnership with us to gain freedom and transformation?

6. What can you and your church do to help shed light on the issue of overcoming sexual sin?

7. After reading this chapter, what is one thing you will put into practice or one thing you will change in your life?

8. How can we, as a group, help you do this?

-CHAPTER 13-

Mt. Doubt

"The de-Santafication process has begun! The de-Santafication process has begun!"[1]

Over and over my ringtone quoting this funny line from "The Santa Clause 2" rang, as the alarm tried desperately to get me out of bed. For fifteen minutes I let it play over and over until my sister, who was down the hall, couldn't stand it anymore and came into my room to turn it off.

Then, three minutes later, alarm number two goes off. (Like you never needed to set two alarms in case the first one didn't do the job!) The second alarm was my favorite motivational song, "Eye of the Tiger." (Hey, if you need a second alarm, you better make it something that will stir your passion and resolve!) But this day, not even the infamous Rocky anthem was doing the job! I didn't have the eye of the tiger, nor was I thrilled with the fight that morning!

Why was I so difficult to rouse this morning? Was it because I had stayed up too late the night before watching football? Was it because the room was so cold and the covers were so warm? Was it sheer laziness? Actually, the answer is none of the above.

The truthful answer was I had wrestled with physical pain the entire night before in bed, and waking up to pain at the level I had was just too overwhelming.

Now, you need to understand that every day I live in physical pain...every step I take on my bad right foot feels like someone is sticking a knife into my foot. However, some days are worse than others, and, having come off one of the bad days only to wake up to more instant pain, I didn't have the fight to get up and face another day.

Difficult times don't go away the day we get saved. Our lives don't become all candy canes and gumdrops when we begin to follow God. This is a tough truth to hear, but it is true.

• People still face tough times.

• People still have physical pain.

• Financial issues still surround us.

• Relationships don't always go the way we want.

• Tough times don't just vanish.

Life is full of struggles, hardships, trials, and tribulations. These difficulties can cause us to take refuge in the shade of Mt. Doubt, wondering if God will come through and help us. Often, they leave us staggering from their mighty blow. That morning when my alarm rang and rang, I had to make a choice...I could continue to hide under the covers, or rally and endure. Thankfully, God helped me find the strength to get up and face another day through his help.

This instance reminded me of one of my favorite stories in the Bible. The man we are going to look at is an excellent model of how to handle the difficulties and trying times we face. His story shows us not only how to handle difficult times that cause us to doubt God, but it also shows us one of the most honest prayers in the Bible. It's found in Mark 9.

Mark 9 begins with Jesus, James, John, and Peter climbing to the top of a high mountain.

> *After six days Jesus took Peter, James, and John with Him and led them up a high mountain, where they were all alone. There He was transfigured before them. His clothes became dazzling white, whiter than anyone in the world could bleach them. And there appeared before them Elijah and Moses, who were talking with Jesus.*
>
> *Peter said to Jesus, "Rabbi, it is good for us to be here. Let us put up three shelters—one for you, one for Moses and one for Elijah." (He did not know what to say, they were so frightened.)*
>
> *Then a cloud appeared and covered them, and a voice came from the cloud: "This is my Son, whom I love. Listen to him!"*
>
> *Suddenly, when they looked around, they no longer saw anyone with them except Jesus. Mark 9:2-8, (NIV)*

It was a spectacular display to see and an awe-inspiring, holy experience. On the mountain, far away from the people and difficulties that constantly surrounded them, these men saw Jesus transfigured. Then Moses and Elijah come down from Heaven and spoke to Jesus, and they heard the voice of God speak and tell them to listen to Jesus.

It had to be tempting to want to never leave such a time of God's presence, but there were people at the foot of the mountain who still needed Jesus' help. Life's problems, trials and tribulations were still going on below. So Jesus and the three disciples made the descent back down the mountain. It is at the foot of the mountain that we meet the man we are going to study. He is going through a horrific problem that would devastate most. He needed Jesus to help his son!

> *When they came to the other disciples, they saw a large crowd around them and the teachers of the law arguing with them. As soon as all the people saw Jesus, they were overwhelmed with wonder and ran to greet Him. "What are you arguing with them about?" He asked. A man in the crowd answered, "Teacher, I*

> *brought you my son, who is possessed by a spirit that has robbed him of speech. Whenever it seizes him, it throws him to the ground. He foams at the mouth, gnashes his teeth and becomes rigid. I asked Your disciples to drive out the spirit, but they could not." "You unbelieving generation," Jesus replied, "how long shall I stay with you? How long shall I put up with you? Bring the boy to me." Mark 9:14-19 (NIV)*

What a tragic situation! This man had to watch his son be attacked, overcome, and mutilated by this demon, and there was no way he could help him.

It is obvious that this has been going on for some time. Now he came to Jesus for help.

However, Jesus was gone when he came to the disciples, and, although the disciples were doing the best they could, they could do little to help. Actually, it seems they made it worse, because the demon came on the boy and made him convulse again.

> *When the spirit saw Jesus, it immediately threw the boy into a convulsion. He fell to the ground and rolled around, foaming at the mouth.*
>
> *Jesus asked the boy's father, "How long has he been like this?"*
>
> *"From childhood," he answered. "It has often thrown him into fire or water to kill him. But if you can do anything, take pity on us and help us." Mark 9:20-22 (NIV)*

This man's heart is breaking. He can't take anymore. As many of us do, He cries out to Jesus for help. However, he asks for help in a questioning way. There is some doubt in the question. This fact didn't go unnoticed by Jesus. Look at verse 23:

> *"If you can?" said Jesus. "Everything is possible for one who believes." (NIV)*

These words touched the man deeply and he uttered what I believe is the most honest prayer in the Bible. Look at verse 24:

Immediately the boy's father exclaimed, "I do believe; help me overcome my unbelief!" (NIV)

What an honest statement!

Anyone who has ever gone through a hard time can relate to what this man said. He KNOWS Jesus has the power to set His Son free. Yet disappointment and the pain of our experiences make us wonder IF God will help us.

This man believed, yet he was tired and emotionally drained. In this state of mind, he wondered if Jesus would help him. Jesus' words to him stirred some hope, and he knew he needed help conquering Mt. Doubt to grab hold of this hope, so he confessed his faith and asked Jesus to give him the hope and strength to continue believing.

We KNOW Jesus has the power to set us free. Yet disappointment and the pain of our experiences make us wonder IF God will help us.

I love the fact that Jesus doesn't rebuke this man for his statement. Jesus understood the man's heartache. He related to his emotional exhaustion. He looked at the man with compassion. Jesus knew the man believed He could help him. So He spoke the words needed to strengthen his faith. The man's prayer showed he was fully relying on Jesus to give him the strength to continue believing. As a result, He saw his son miraculously delivered and set free.

When Jesus saw that a crowd was running to the scene, He rebuked the impure spirit. "You deaf and mute spirit," He said, "I command you, come out of him and never enter him again."

The spirit shrieked, convulsed him violently and came out. The boy looked so much like a corpse that many said, "He's dead."

But Jesus took him by the hand and lifted him to his feet, and he stood up.

Jesus didn't condemn the father for his doubt and unbelief. Instead, he rewarded the man for his honesty about his unbelief. He acknowledged the man's faith amidst the struggle, and he healed his son!

This man serves as a model for us all of how we should handle our times of difficulty and doubt. I can't tell you how many times I have personally prayed this prayer. I was able to get out of bed that day I mentioned in the beginning of the chapter by praying this prayer. It wasn't the first time. It won't be the last.

Right now in my own life, I am fighting a huge battle with doubt. I am writing this chapter to help my own spirit just as much as yours. A little over a year ago, I was given the honor of being appointed as an Assemblies of God US Missionary Associate with Church Planters and Developers with the commission of helping churches develop men's ministries. While a great blessing, it came with a huge mountain to climb.

You see, part of this involves raising my mission's budget. Just like a missionary who goes overseas has to raise their full support budget, I, too, have to raise my financial support. I had to give up the ability to be bi-vocational or have other sources of income. All I am permitted to earn is money raised through this budget.

It has been a terrifying process. I have struggled with doubt through this process like I never have before. What if I can't raise the money? What if God doesn't provide? Can I trust God to come through for me?

I have spent many nights lying in bed struggling with these questions.

I know God has the ability and power to help me, but when I am beat up and exhausted by the pain and hardships of life, my faith wavers, and I think that God won't help me and I'll be stuck in my situation forever.

It is a continuing battle where I have had to pray this man's prayer and say to God:

"I believe You can help me. I believe You have the power to provide for me. I believe Your power can get me through this. However, I have a hard time believing You are going to help me. I struggle thinking You are going to let me down. I doubt You will come through for me. Father, I believe, but please help my unbelief!"

You see, it's the "will," not the "can" that doubt torments us with. I know God can help me, but the doubt makes me ask *"will He help me?"*

This is when I need to turn to God more than ever and beg Him to help me conquer Mt. Doubt.

It's the "will," not the "can" that doubt torments us with. We know God can help us, but the doubt makes us ask "will He help us?"

Often, God finds ways to strengthen my faith. I'll hear a song, read a verse in the Bible, or someone will encourage me. God always finds a way to help my unbelief.

I often find myself thanking God for inspiring Mark to put this man's prayer in the Bible. It truly is an amazing and honest prayer, and it serves as an excellent model of how to pray during hard and difficult times.

What about you?

Do you have a relationship that makes your faith waver?

Do you deal with a physical infirmity that some days wears you down and makes you think God isn't going to help you through?

Are you a parent wrestling in the Heavenlies for the soul of your child, scared they won't turn back to God?

Are you struggling financially, and are fearful that God won't keep His word to supply your needs?

Have you lost your job and struggle to believe God will supply a new job for you?

Does doubt ever leave you thinking, "God is never going to help me?"

Does the situation you are in seem hopeless?

Do you feel God is unable to set you free?

Are you feeling overwhelmed?

Has the pain and heartache of your situation left you struggling for help?

Is Mt. Doubt standing in front of you, scaring you into staying put and not trusting God?

I understand the hardships and exhaustion this brings. I encourage you to pray the prayer that this father prayed.

Tell God you believe He has the power to help you, but the burden you are carrying causes you to doubt that He WILL help you. Ask Him for hope and encouragement to continue on. I am sure this is a prayer God will answer. He did it for this father, and He has done it for me. He will do it for you, too.

Has this chapter tugged at your heart?

Have you read this and thought, *"Jamie, I am there! I am struggling so hard to continue trusting and believing God. Life is kicking me around, and I don't know if I can go on. I KNOW God can help me, but I am TERRIFIED He won't."*

If that's you, it's time to rise up and fight Mt. Doubt.

Victory begins with this prayer. It ends when you give it to God and allow Him to bring you through.

Dear Heavenly Father,

You know the trial and hardship I am going through, Father, I believe You have the strength and power to move mightily in my life, yet the emotional exhaustion I am feeling causes me to doubt You will help me. Father, I pray the same prayer as this brave father prayed, "I believe, help my unbelief."

Give me the hope and strength to continue forward. Provide me with the encouragement I need to keep trusting in You. Father, strengthen my faith in You. In Jesus' name, Amen.

GROUP STUDY QUESTIONS:

1. How does doubt attack you?

2. We said, *"It is the 'will' not the 'can' that doubt torments us with."* How is this true in your life?

3. Doubt tries to make us think God won't help us, but, rationally, why wouldn't God help you?

4. How can you run towards God during times of doubt?

5. After reading this chapter, what is one thing you will put into practice or one thing you will change in your life?

6. How can we, as a group, help you do this?

-CHAPTER 14-

LIVING IN YOUR PROMISED LAND

We are coming to the end of our time together. Hopefully, this book has inspired you to start climbing your own mountains. My wish for you is that you conquer these mountains so you can enter into your Promised Land. Why?

The answer to this is simple…because, while it is crucial for you to climb your mountain so you can experience the freedom and victory that God has called you to, it isn't just for your freedom. Other people's freedom depends on it as well. What do I mean?

God desires for us to take our newfound freedom, joy, peace, and victory and help others experience the same freedom. Just like God used my story to help you climb your mountains, he wants to take your story, your past, your defeats, and your victories to help inspire others to conquer their mountains.

I believe wholeheartedly that, once you conquer the mountains in your life, God will bring other hurting people into your path. They will share with you their hurts, pains, struggles, and battles. They will say to you, *"I just don't think I can go forward any further."*

This will be the moment when your experience climbing the mountain will come shining through. You will be able to say to them, *"I know what you're going through. I understand how high the mountains seem. I get that it seems impossible to climb. I've been where you are.*

God will use your mountain experience to help another hurting person climb to the top.

Yes, the mountains seem big, but my God is bigger! He helped me conquer this mountain, and I know He can do the same in your life!"

God will use your mountain experience to help another hurting person climb to the top.

He will use you to reach down and give them the hand they need to reach the summit with you.

He will use you to help them enter into their Promised Land. And God's kingdom will grow stronger.

Just yesterday, my coach said to me, *"Jamie, you have learned how to make defeat your fuel."* What he was saying was what I described above. God will take your mountain, your obstacle, the thing that was once your defeat, and He will make your defeat your fuel. He will use you to help others break free of their mountains.

God will take your mountain, your obstacle, the thing that was once your defeat, and he will make your defeat your fuel.

I repeat the command we started the book off with so many pages ago:

You have stayed at your mountain too long!

God has a great life ready and waiting for you. He will give you victory, and He will use your testimony to help others.

There is no mountain, no sin, no bondage, and no stronghold that the power of God can't overcome. Freedom is yours. You are invincible through the power of God. But to experience this freedom, you have to first choose to leave your mountain behind and follow God into your Promised Land.

Others are depending on you to reach the top! Will you climb?

As we end this journey together, instead of me giving you a prayer to pray, I want to close by praying for you.

Dear Heavenly Father,

Thank You for all the work You have done in my life to help me leave the safety and security of my mountains. Thank You for helping me to conquer them and move into Your Promised Land. I truly know I do not deserve the blessings You have given to me. Thank You for taking my story and using it to help others.

Father, please help everyone who reads this book realize they too can conquer their mountains. Help them see they don't have to stay defeated, stuck in the shadow of the sins and mistakes of their past, or the hurts and pains others have thrown onto them. Give them a supernatural perseverance and drive to conquer their mountains.

Help them truly see that, through the power of the Holy Spirit, they are invincible! Nothing can stop them. No sin can bind them! Victory is theirs! Help them leave the mountain and climb into the freedom and victory that comes only through You.

Then use them to help other people experience the same freedom. Help them lift up these other hurting people and conquer their mountains. Build an army of invincible men, ready to live in Your freedom, an army that can scale their mountains!

In Jesus' Name, AMEN!

GROUP STUDY QUESTIONS:

1. Which mountain discussed in this book have you experienced the greatest victory over?

2. How can God use this victory to help another person?

3. Who can you help come to the realization that they are invincible and can conquer their own mountains?

4. After reading this book, what is the most important thing you would like to put into practice or one thing you will change in your life?

5. How can we, as a group, help you do this?

WORKBOOK

-CHAPTER ONE-

You've Stayed Here Too Long!

- Too many of God's men came to Christ, accepted his salvation, but have yet to experience the complete _____ they can have in Christ. Their _____ are keeping them from moving forward.

- We as humans tolerate our _____ and our way too much! Freedom is there for us, but we decide to just accept things as they are. But God is calling us to more! He is saying, "You have _____ at your mountain too long."

What is the mountain in your life that is keeping you from moving forward into your Promised Land?

CONTRACT BETWEEN YOU AND GOD

(AND YOUR MEN'S GROUP IF WORKING TOGETHER AS A GROUP)

Will you commit to:

Reading each chapter, including Scripture verses? Yes / No

Praying the prayers at the end of the chapter? Yes / No

Sincerely examining your heart using the questions at the end of each chapter? Yes / No

I,_____, am committed to

conquering the mountains that keep me from freedom. I affirm this

decision with my signature.

_____   _____

(Sign)   (Date)

GROUP STUDY QUESTIONS:

1. Which mountain listed in the chapter jumped out to you the most?

2. Why do you think we tolerate our mountains and our frogs?

3. Are you willing to commit to climbing your mountains?

4. What spoke to you the most in this chapter?

5. After reading this chapter, what is one thing you will put into practice or one thing you will change in your life?

6. How can we, as a group, help you do this?

–CHAPTER TWO–

MT. FEAR

• _____ are areas where Satan has established control. They are areas of frequent

that are so strong they result in feelings of failure, hopelessness, and defeat.

• God's will is for you to break the grip _____ has on you and embrace his _____.

List three fears you have faced in your life:

1.

2.

3.

What caused these fears?

1.

2.

3.

Write down three Bible verses you can memorize to help combat your fears:

1.

2.

3.

GROUP STUDY QUESTIONS:

1. What is an area of fear that keeps you from moving forward?

2. What is a stronghold? Can you recognize any strongholds in your life?

3. When did your fear start? What caused it?

4. How can prayer and Bible reading help you conquer Mt. Fear?

5. After reading this chapter, what is one thing you will put into practice or one thing you will change in your life?

6. How can we, as a group, help you do this?

-CHAPTER THREE-

MT. SICKNESS

- We can't _____ our disability, sickness, or disease, but we can change how we _____ to it and allow it to influence our lives.

- Very few people will _____ _____ on a disabled person or refuse to be around them or like them…however, likes being around a bitter person!

- God _____ heal you if it is best for his kingdom and he heal you if it isn't the best thing for his kingdom. It isn't about _____, it's about _____.

- When you make your greatest _____ into God's greatest _____ through you, lives will be _____, and God's kingdom will _____.

How have sicknesses or physical issues affected your life?

How can you keep your sickness from being your identity?

Write down three ways God could use your physical issues to grow his Kingdom, (if not your own, then think of someone else):

1.

2.

3.

How has your sickness affected your relationship with God? Was it in a good way or a bad way?

GROUP STUDY QUESTIONS:

1. In this chapter, we said, *"Be a victor, not a victim."* What did this mean to you?

2. Why is removing bitterness important to climbing Mt. Sickness?

3. How can God use your weakness to build his kingdom?

4. How can prayer and Bible reading help you conquer Mt. Sickness?

5. After reading this chapter, what is one thing you will put into practice or one thing you will change in your life?

6. How can we, as a group, help you do this?

–CHAPTER FOUR–

MT. ABUSE

- Talking breaks the cycle of _____, and
are the ropes that hold abusive relationships together.

- It's only as we begin to see ourselves through the eyes of our

_____ _____ and find our

in Him that we begin to understand that we don't deserve to be

abused.

Have you faced abuse in your life? Describe it below:

Identify three people you can ask to be your support system:

1.

2.

3.

Write out three Bible passages that can help you break the grip of abuse in your life:

1.

2.

3.

Why is it important to forgive your abuser?

GROUP STUDY QUESTIONS:

1. Why is it important to break the silence to conquer abuse?

2. We said in this chapter that it is possible to get so familiar with abuse that you can actually crave it. Why do you think this is, and what does this mean to you?

3. Why is it important to understand how God feels about you to conquer abuse?

4. Who can be your support system to help you defeat abuse in your life?

5. After reading this chapter, what is one thing you will put into practice or one thing you will change in your life?

6. How can we, as a group, help you do this?

–CHAPTER FIVE–

MT. ANGER

- John puts it quite bluntly, if you _____ someone, you're not _____ under the influence of God.

- If you're _____ your wife and kids, I'll go so far as to say you're in spiritual trouble…you need to turn to God and _____ and start again.

- Forgiveness is not an _____. It is a _____ you need to make.

What is the Anger Spiral?

1.

2.

3.

What is the source of your anger? When did it start?

What is keeping you from forgiving?

What steps can you take to begin forgiving?

1.

2.

3.

GROUP STUDY QUESTIONS:

1. We said that most abusive anger starts as hatred. What are your thoughts on this?

2. Why does hate cause separation between us and God?

3. Discuss this statement: *"If you're hitting your wife and kids, I'll go so far as to say you're in spiritual trouble, you need to turn to God and repent and start again."*

4. What is something nice you can do for the person you need to forgive?

5. After reading this chapter, what is one thing you will put into practice or one thing you will change in your life?

6. How can we, as a group, help you do this?

-CHAPTER SIX-

MT. SHAME

- Shame…comes in all _____ and
  and clings to people of all _____ and
  _____.

- When you are constantly being barraged with bombshells from an
  enemy, you are _____   _____.
  When you decide to _____ _____---you are at
  _____.

- Knowing all of your faults and flaws, shortcomings and weaknesses,
  God still _____ you.

- Satan has _____ _____ to use the weapon of shame
  against you. You are a _____ _____, living
  a _____ _____.

In what area does shame attack you?

How does God see you?

To deal a death-blow to shame, write down your testimony:

GROUP STUDY QUESTIONS:

1. We said that *"Shame is a sense deep inside that there is something fundamentally wrong with you."* How would you define shame?

2. Why is important to understand that shame is an attack from the enemy?

3. Why is knowing and memorizing verses of how God sees you important to conquering shame?

4. Why is it important to get to the root cause of our shame?

5. How does sharing your testimony help defeat shame?

6. After reading this chapter, what is one thing you will put into practice or one thing you will change in your life?

7. How can we, as a group, help you do this?

–CHAPTER SEVEN–

MT. FAILURE

- Failure is not an _____, it's a _____.

- During your time of failure, don't just sit around waiting for it to be over—_____ all you can. The more you the more you are able to invest in _____ _____.

What is your biggest failure in life?

What new skills can you learn during this time of failure to prepare you for the future?

1.

2.

3.

Why is it important to spend time in prayer and in God's Word during a time of failure?

What are three steps you can take to conquer failure in your life?

1.

2.

3.

GROUP STUDY QUESTIONS:

1. What have you failed at in life?

2. How has this failure shaped your life?

3. Why is it important to allow God to heal your heart after failure?

4. How can we enjoy our life during times of failure?

5. After reading this chapter, what is one thing you will put into practice or one thing you will change in your life?

6. How can we, as a group, help you do this?

–CHAPTER EIGHT–

MT. BETRAYAL

• We cannot react in a _____ or

way. We cannot try and _____ our attacker or

_____ _____ for the evil they have done to us. This

is the action of a carnal man, and we are men following God.

• When dealing with a betrayer, the hardest thing in the world to do

is to not _____ _____ with evil. Yet,

this is what God calls us to do.

• _____ holds us in bondage and captive

to our betrayers. However, when we forgive them, we free

_____from their actions. So we need to

forgive them.

Who has betrayed you in life? Describe it below:

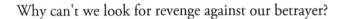

Why can't we look for revenge against our betrayer?

List two good things you can do for this betrayer:

1.

2.

What scares you about forgiving your betrayer? How does this line up with God's Word?

GROUP STUDY QUESTIONS:

1. Why can't we get back at or take revenge against someone who betrays us?

2. What good thing can you do for your betrayer?

3. Why is it sometimes necessary to let the relationship go?

4. Which part of our discussion on forgiveness stood out the most to you?

5. After reading this chapter, what is one thing you will put into practice or one thing you will change in your life?

6. How can we, as a group, help you do this?

–Chapter Nine–

Mt. Broken Relationships

- Healing starts with _____ we have a

  _____ .

- If you _____ the relationship, there is hope. It will

  take a lot of hard work on your part, but God can

  the relationship

- If you are the one who was hurt, you must _____ .

_____ is about setting yourself free to experience

God's love and healing regardless of what happens to the other

person.

Who do you have a broken relationship with? Were you the relationship breaker or breakee?

IF YOU ARE THE BREAKER:

Why is it important to admit you caused the problem?

What are three changes you can make to your life to help rebuild trust?

1.

2.

3.

IF YOU ARE THE BREAKEE:

What is keeping you from forgiving the person who broke the relationship?

Are you willing to rebuild the relationship? Are you willing to accept that the relationship may not be able to be restored?

GROUP STUDY QUESTIONS:

1. Do you have a broken relationship in your life?

2. Were you responsible for breaking the relationship?

3. Why is it important to seek forgiveness?

4. Why is it important to rebuild trust and to give the other person time to heal?

5. Which part of our discussion on forgiveness stood out the most to you?

6. After reading this chapter, what is one thing you will put into practice or one thing you will change in your life?

7. How can we, as a group, help you do this?

-CHAPTER TEN-

MT. DEBT

- _____ and numbers aren't the problems...our actions, attitudes, and spending habits are the _____.

- Debt is a _____ issue.

- The biggest risk to using _____ _____ is sinking in debt and losing everything you worked hard to accomplish. Do you know what the biggest risk to only using

  is? _____ _____!

- If you stop using credit, develop a plan, and commit yourself to sticking to it, there will come a day when your

  will be _____ ____ _____.

What is your appetite, the thing that you have to have that causes you to have debt?

Identify who can help you be financially accountable:

How does God view debt?

What has kept you from living on a budget?

What action will you take to start a budget?

GROUP STUDY QUESTIONS:

1. This chapter says: *"Money and numbers aren't the problems...our actions, attitudes, and spending habits are the problem."* What does this mean?

2. What appetite do you have that contributes to your debt?

3. When do your appetites cause you to spend money?

4. How does God feel about debt?

5. Do you live on a budget? If not, why? Will you commit to developing a budget?

6. After reading this chapter, what is one thing you will put into practice or one thing you will change in your life?

7. How can we, as a group, help you do this?

–CHAPTER ELEVEN–

MT. GRIEF

- Don't cut off your _____ _____ _____ to ease the pain. It doesn't ease it, it just _____ it. And slowly, it kills your spirit. You've stayed at Mt. Grief too long!

- We need to _____ our will to the Divine will and accept that He controls even the things that we do not _____.

- Remember that this is only a _____ in our lives. You will not always be _____. You will not always be _____ _____ in life. Eventually, your new life will become your normal life.

Who or what have you lost in your life? How has grief affected your life?

How has guilt contributed to your grief?

What are three ways you can start climbing Mt. Grief?

1.

2.

3.

GROUP STUDY QUESTIONS:

1. What has caused grief in your life?

2. How can we balance not avoiding grief with not staying at Mt. Grief for too long?

3. How can guilt trap us in grief?

4. How can you run towards God during times of grief?

5. After reading this chapter, what is one thing you will put into practice or one thing you will change in your life?

6. How can we, as a group, help you do this?

–Chapter Twelve–

Mt. Porn

- You need to find a _____,
  believer and tell them about your struggle. The light of
  burns away the darkness of _____.

- Sex is meant for the _____ _____,
  not a _____ _____ in front of a computer screen.

- It is better to lose _____ temporarily than to lose your
  _____ eternally.

- We cannot yield to sensuality and pornography if we are

  _____ from it. _____ for your life.

How is pornography sinning against God?

Identify who you can confess your struggle with pornography to:

What four steps can you take to conquer pornography in your life?

1.

2.

3.

4.

GROUP STUDY QUESTIONS:

1. What are some sexual triggers that people are susceptible to?

2. When are you most vulnerable to sexual temptation?

3. What are several ways of escape you will utilize when you become aware you're being tempted?

4. Why is having an accountability partner important? What are the two most important questions you'd advise an accountability partner to ask you when you meet?

5. What is our role in partnership with the power of the Holy Spirit to gain freedom and transformation? What is the Holy Spirit's role in partnership with us to gain freedom and transformation?

6. What can you and your church do to help shed light on the issue of overcoming sexual sin?

7. After reading this chapter, what is one thing you will put into practice or one thing you will change in your life?

8. How can we, as a group, help you do this?

-CHAPTER THIRTEEN-

MT. DOUBT

- The father _____ Jesus has the power to set His Son free. Yet disappointment and the pain of our experiences make us wonder _____ God will help us.

- It's the "_____," not the "_____" that doubt torments us with. I _____ God can help me, but the doubt makes me ask "_____ _____ help me?"

How does doubt attack you?

How does your fear and doubt line up with God's Word?

Write out three Bible verses to help you battle doubt:

1.

2.

3.

GROUP STUDY QUESTIONS:

1. How does doubt attack you?

2. We said, *"It is the will, not the can that doubt torments us with."* How is this true in your life?

3. Why wouldn't God help you?

4. How can you run towards God during times of doubt?

5. After reading this chapter, what is one thing you will put into practice or one thing you will change in your life?

6. How can we, as a group, help you do this?

-CHAPTER FOURTEEN-

LIVING IN YOUR PROMISED LAND

- God will use your mountain experience to help another

  _____ climb to the top.

- God will take your mountain, your obstacle, the thing that was

  once your defeat, and he will make your _____ your

  _____.

- There is no mountain, no sin, no bondage, and no stronghold that

  the _____ of God can't _____.

What mountains have you gained freedom from throughout this study?

How can you make defeat your fuel?

GROUP STUDY QUESTIONS:

1. Which mountain discussed in this book have you experienced the greatest victory over?

2. How can God use this victory to help another person?

3. Who can you help come to the realization that they are invincible and can conquer their own mountains?

4. After reading this book, what is the most important thing you would like to put into practice or one thing you will change in your life?

5. How can we, as a group, help you do this?

FILL IN ANSWERS

Chapter 1
• freedom, mountains
• mountains, frogs, stayed

Chapter 2
• Strongholds, temptations
• fear, freedom

Chapter 3
• change, react
• look down, NO ONE
• will, won't, you, Him
• weakness, strength, changed, grow

Chapter 4
• secrets, secrets
• Heavenly Father, identity

Chapter 5
• hate, walking
• hitting, repent
• emotion, mental decision

Chapter 6
• shapes, sizes, backgrounds, cultures
• under attack, fight back, war
• God, chose
• no right, new creation, new life

Chapter 7
• end, detour
• learn, learn, God's Kingdom

Chapter 8
• vengeful, hateful, destroy, pay them back
• repay evil
• Unforgiveness, ourselves

Chapter 9
• admitting, problem
• broke, restore
• forgive, Forgiveness

Chapter 10
• Money, problem
• heart
• credit cards, cash, Paper cuts
• debt, paid in full

Chapter 11
• heart and emotions, buries
• resurrender, understand
• season, grieving, starting over

Chapter 12
• Trustworthy, Mature, confession, sin
• marriage bed, dark room
• Google, soul
• running away, Run

Chapter 13
• KNOWS, IF
• will, can, know, will He

Chapter 14
• hurting person
• defeat, fuel
• power, overcome

Bibliography

Chapter 2:

1. Bethel Music, "No Longer Slaves." *We Will Not Be Shaken, by:* Brian Johnson, Joel Case, Jonathan David Helser, 2014. Bethel Music Publishing, 2015. CD.

2. Weber, Laverne; *"Victory's Journey"*; Easton, PA: Laverne Weber Ministries, 2017.

Chapter 5:

1. The Avengers, Joss Whedon, Paramount Pictures, Marvel Studios, 2012. Film.

Chapter 6:

1. http://www.verywell.com/what-is-shame-425328

Chapter 7:

1. "Denis Waitley Quotes." BrainyQuote.com. Xplore Inc, 2017. 5 October 2017. https://www.brainyquote.com/quotes/quotes/d/deniswaitl125740.html

2. Woodsen, John. *"They Call Me Coach."* New York, NY: McGraw Hill Companies, 2004.

Chapter 8:

1. Edersheim, Alfred; *"The Life and Times of Jesus the Messiah,"* Grand Rapids, MI: Wm. B. Eerdmans, 1953. Public Domain.

Chapter 10:

1. Ramsey, Dave. *"The Total Money Makeover: A Proven Plan for*

Financial Fitness". Nashville, TN: Thomas Nelson, 2007.

2. John C. Maxwell, Source: quoted by Dave Ramsey in *The Total Money Makeover.*

3. Ramsey, Dave. *"The Total Money Makeover: A Proven Plan for Financial Fitness".* Nashville, TN:Thomas Nelson, 2007.

Chapter 11:

1. The Dark Knight Rises; Christopher Nolan; Warner Bros., DC Entertainment; 2012. Film.

Chapter 12:

1. Presley, Elvis. *"You Gave Me A Mountain"*; Aloha from Hawaii Via Satellite. by: Marty Robbins, 1973, Produced by: Jimmy Bowen, 1973; RCA Records. Vinyl.

Chapter 13:

1. The Santa Clause 2; Michael Lembeck; Walt Disney Pictures, 2006. Film.

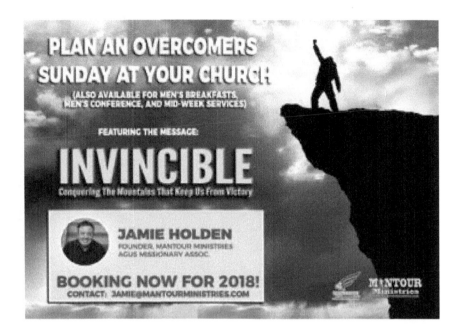
Jamie loves to speak to men and is available to speak at your next men's event. Jamie combines humor and his personal testimony to both engage and challenge men to grow in their walk with God. He uses his testimony of overcoming abuse as well as dealing with his physical and emotional issues growing up to encourage men that no matter what their background or where they have come from in life, they can grow into mighty men in God's kingdom.

"Years ago, while I was attending the University of Valley Forge, God gave me a deep desire to minister to men. My calling is to help men learn what it means to be a godly man and how to develop a deep, personal relationship with their heavenly Father. We strive to challenge and encourage men to reach their full potential in God's kingdom."

If you are interested in having Jamie at your next men's event as a speaker or workshop leader, or if you are interested in having him come share with your church, e-mail him at jamie@mantourministries.com. He is also available to speak for one or multiple weeks on the theme of his books, Putting On Manhood, Legacy: Living a Life that Lasts, Get in the Game, and Invincible.

ALSO AVAILABLE FROM MANTOUR MINISTRIES

AVAILABLE IN PRINT AND DIGITAL FORMATS. VISIT WWW.MANTOURMINISTRIES.COM FOR MORE INFORMATION.

THE MANTOUR GUY

PODCAST

Helping men grow in their walk with God.

MANTOUR
Ministries
www.mantourministries.com

Partner with the Ministry:

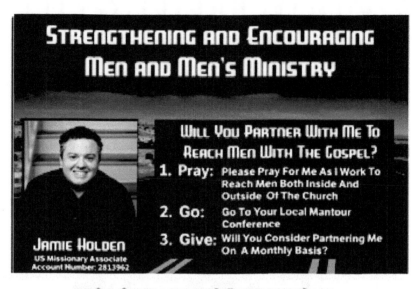

Missionary Faith Promise

Assemblies of God U.S. Missions • 1445 N. Boonville Ave • Springfield, MO 65802-1894
Phone: 417.862.2781 ext. 3264 • Fax: 417.873.9734 • E-mail: AGUSMFinance@ag.org

DONOR INFORMATION

☐ Church   ☐ Individual

Name_____

Address_____

City_____ State_____ Zip_____

Email_____ Tel_____

Account Number:_____

☐ Check here if you do not wish to receive promotional materials from U.S. Missions

CREDIT/DEBIT CARD

Account Number_____ Exp. Date_____

☐ One-time   ☐ Monthly

Amount of Contribution_____

Authorized Signature_____

For non-swiped Character Code_____

MISSIONARY INFORMATION

As the Lord enables us, we promise to invest $_____ each month for support of:

Missionary __**Jamie Holden**__

Account # __**2813962**__   Department __**Missionary Church Planters & Developers**__

Donor Signature_____ Date_____

IMPORTANT: Please keep this missionary a priority. Sign, date and mail this form today along with your first check. God Bless You!

U.S. MISSIONS
that none perish

FORWARD TO AGUSM

PURCHASE A BOOK FOR A PRISONER

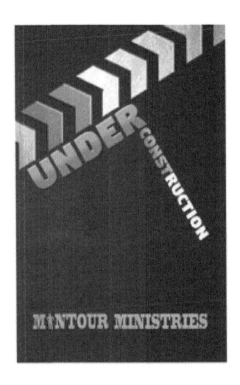

If you enjoyed this book, why not buy a copy
for a man in prison. You can help us reach more
men behind bars by donating at
mantourministries.com.

Mantour Ministries donates copies of our
curriculum to state and federal prisons.
We are reaching men behind bars with the gospel!